Praise for *101 Best Beginnings Ever Written*

"A book as wise and companionable as its author, and a superb resource for writer, student and literary bystander alike. Bravo! Ole!"

—Christopher Buckley, political satirist and the author of
God Is My Broker, Thank You for Smoking, and other novels.

"This book successfully serves two purposes. For a writer it may inspire and instruct how best to begin a story or novel. For the layman this book provides a GPS through literature, driving us to the novels we simply must read soon."

—Sol Stein, author of *Stein on Writing* and several novels and plays.

Other Books by Barnaby Conrad

Nonfiction

La Fiesta Brava

Gates of Fear

The Death of Manolete

San Francisco: A Profile in Words and Pictures

Famous Last Words

Tahiti

Encyclopedia of Bullfighting

How to Fight a Bull

Fun While It Lasted

A Revolting Transaction

Time Is All We Have

Hemingway's Spain

The Complete Guide to Writing Fiction

Name Dropping

Snoopy's Guide to the Writing Life (with Monte Schulz)

The World of Herb Caen

Learning to Write Fiction from the Masters

Santa Barbara

The 101 Best Scenes Ever Written

Fiction

The Innocent Villa

Matador

Dangerfield

Zorro: A Fox in the City

Endangered (with Niels Mortensen)

Fire Below Zero (with Nico Mastorakis)

Keepers of the Secret (with Nico Mastorakis)

Last Boat to Cadiz

Translations

The Wounds of Hunger (Spoto)

The Second Life of Captain Contreras (Luca de Tena)

My Life as a Matador (Autobiography of Carlos Arruza)

101 Best Beginnings Ever Written

A Romp Through Literary Openings
for Writers and Readers!

Barnaby Conrad

Fresno, California

Printed in the United States of America

Published by Quill Driver Books
an imprint of Linden Publishing
2006 S. Mary
Fresno, California 93721
559-233-6633 / 800-345-4447
QuillDriverBooks.com

Quill Driver Books and Colophon are trademarks of
Linden Publishing, Inc.
Printed in the United States of America

Quill Driver Books' titles may be purchased in quantity at special
discounts for educational, fund-raising, business, or promotional use.
Please contact Special Markets, Quill Driver Books,
at the above address or at **559-233-6633**.

To order another copy of this book, please call
1-800-345-4447.

Quill Driver Books Project Cadre:
Christine Hernandez, Steve Mettee, Maura J. Zimmer, Kent Sorsky,
John David Marion, Doris Hall

ISBN: 978-1-884956-86-7 (1-884956-86-6)

135798642

Library of Congress Cataloging-in-Publication Data
Conrad, Barnaby, 1922-
    101 best beginnings ever written : a romp through literature's most titillating,
intriguing, and exciting openers for writers and readers / by Barnaby Conrad.
        p. cm.
    ISBN 978-1-884956-86-7 (1-884956-86-6)
    1. Openings (Rhetoric) 2. Fiction--Technique. I. Title. II. Title: One hundred
one best beginnings ever written. III. Title: One hundred and one best beginnings ever
written.
    PN3383.O64C66 2008
    808.3--dc22
                                2008037061

"It's none of their business that you have to learn to write. Let them think you were born that way."

—From an interview with Ernest Hemingway

A Note to My Readers

When I was twenty-five years old, I worked for America's first Nobel Prize winner, Sinclair Lewis, for six months as chauffeur-secretary-verbal punching bag, and protégé. He was the wealthiest and most famous American writer at that time. I learned a great deal about writing from him, especially about the importance of The Beginning.

"I once got a shocking visual example of just how important it is," he told me once at breakfast at his vast estate in Williamstown, Massachusetts. "It was on the deck of a transatlantic steamer, where I happily saw a lovely young woman in a deck chair pick up my new novel, *The Man Who Knew Coolidge*. I'd never actually seen anyone reading one of my books—it was quite exciting. She opened it to the first page, read for about a minute, then got up, walked to the rail, and dropped my book over the side. I never wrote a boring beginning ever again."

Contents

Preface

We can learn from the masters, old and modern, how to begin a novel or a short story in a way that will catch the reader's (or more important, an editor's) attention. Remember, when an editor takes your piece out of its manila envelope, you will not be there at his elbow to say: "Keep reading! It gets really good later on—*terrific* scene coming up!"

There'll be no "later on" if the editor is not intrigued right off the bat. He or she does not necessarily have to be shocked, startled, or amazed, but the editor, putting himself in the place of a reader, must be tantalized, intrigued, or curious enough to read further. Professional writers seldom write a dull first page of a novel or short story. A well-drafted opening— maybe just the first sentence—immediately tells the editor that he is dealing with a good writer.

Someone asked me the simplistic question recently: Which is more important—a good beginning or a good ending?

I gave the obvious and simplistic answer.

"If you don't have a good beginning, the reader will never get to the ending, no matter how brilliant it might be."

One can learn a great deal about the craft of writing fiction by studying the first pages of great writers.

I have broken beginnings into twelve categories.

What follows are the dozen *basic* ways to begin a story. The ways vary enormously, of course, even within their own categories.

1

Characterization

A CLASSIC WAY TO START A SHORT STORY OR A NOVEL IS WITH A flat-out, no-nonsense description of the protagonist or antagonist.

But it must be very well written.

It should go beyond simply taking the physical inventory of the person, something more, for example, than saying "she had a generous mouth and high cheekbones." (Someday I hope to encounter a story whose heroine has *low* cheekbones!)

Look how much more than just a physical description Annie Proulx gets into the opening of her 2008 *New Yorker* short story, "Tits-Up in a Ditch."

> Her mother had been knockout beautiful and no good, and Dakotah had heard this from the time she could recognize words. People said that Shaina Lister, with aquamarine eyes and curls the shining maroon of waterbirch bark, had won all the kiddie beauty contests and then had become the high-school slut, knocked up when she was fifteen and cutting out the day after Dakotah was born, slinking and wincing, still in her hospital Johnny, down the back stairs of Mercy Maternity to the street, where one of her greasy pals picked her up and headed west for Los Angeles. It was the same day the television evangelist Jim Bakker, an exposed and confessed adulterer, resigned from his Praise the Lord money mill, his fall mourned by Bonita Lister, Shaina's mother. Bonita's husband, Verl, blamed the television for Shaina's wildness and for her hatred of the ranch.

"She seen it was O.K. on the teevee and so she done it," he said. He wanted to get rid of the set, but Bonita said there was no sense in locking up the horse after the barn burned down.

(Incidentally, the female in the title's "ditch" is a cow.)

 හ ❖ ଓ

Here is Dashiell Hammett's beginning to his classic mystery novel, *The Maltese Falcon*:

Samuel Spade's jaw was long and bony, his chin a jutting v under the more flexible v of his mouth. His nostrils curved back to make another, smaller v. His yellow-grey eyes were horizontal. The v motif was picked up again by thickish brows rising outward from twin creases above a hooked nose, and his pale brown hair grew down—from high flat temples—in a point on his forehead. He looked rather pleasantly like a blond satan.

He said to Effie Perine: "Yes, sweetheart?"

She was a lanky sunburned girl whose tan dress of thin woolen stuff clung to her with an effect of dampness. Her eyes were brown and playful in a shiny boyish face. She finished shutting the door behind her, leaned against it, and said: "There's a girl wants to see you. Her name's Wonderly."

"A customer?"

"I guess so. You'll want to see her anyway: she's a knockout."

"Shoo her in, darling," said Spade. "Shoo her in."

Effie Perine opened the door again, following it back into the outer office, standing with a hand on the knob while saying: "Will you come in, Miss Wonderly?"

This beginning, written in 1929, has become a must for the private eye type of story, such as Robert B. Parker's Spenser books, Harlan Coben's Myron Bolitar series, and a host of others. Garrison Keillor's Guy Noir character on his radio show "A Prairie Home Companion" always starts this way, and the parodies are endless:

"I was sitting in my office when this gorgeous blonde slinks in and approaches my desk in installments..." et cetera.

I recently asked Ray Bradbury what was the greatest opening sentence he'd ever read. He barely hesitated: "One that begins with a brilliant succinct character description, Rafael Sabatini's novel *Scaramouche*, which begins: 'He was born with the gift of laughter and a sense that the world was mad.'"

Joseph Conrad's classic novel, *Lord Jim*, published in 1900, begins with a character description, but in a more pedestrian fashion than Sabatini's:

> He was an inch, perhaps two, under six feet, powerfully built, and he advanced straight at you with a slight stoop of the shoulders, head forward, and a fixed-from-under stare which made you think of a charging bull. His voice was deep, loud, and his manner displayed a kind of dogged self-assertion which had nothing aggressive in it. It seemed a necessity, and it was directed apparently as much at himself as at anybody else. He was spotlessly neat, appareled in immaculate white from shoes to hat, and in the various Eastern ports where he got his living as ship-chandler's water-clerk he was very popular.

While apparently a simple description of the way the man appeared to the world, notice how much subtle information we get about his character, his relations with other people, and even his profession.

How different is the beginning of Vladimir Nabokov's flamboyant and scandalous novel, *Lolita*, which begins straight away with an introduction to our eponymous heroine—the *very* young heroine:

> Lolita, light of my life, fire of my loins. My sin, my soul. Lo-lee-ta: the tip of the tongue taking a trip of three steps down the palate to tap, at three, on the teeth. Lo. Lee. Ta.
>
> She was Lo, plain Lo, in the morning, standing four feet ten in one sock. She was Lola in slacks. She was Dolly at school. She was Dolores on the dotted line. But in my arms she was always Lolita.
>
> Did she have a precursor? She did, indeed she did. In point of fact, there might have been no Lolita at all had I not loved,

one summer, a certain initial girl-child. In a princedom by the sea. Oh when? About as many years before Lolita was born as my age was that summer. You can always count on a murderer for a fancy prose style.

Though it starts lightly, frivolously, even gaily, the word "murderer" brings our interest up sharply. Though not without humor, this is a hard-hitting and very dark tale.

ဆာ ❖ ⬠

John Steinbeck starts his story, *The Red Pony*, with a straightforward description of the cowhand of the story:

> At daybreak Billy Buck emerged from the bunkhouse and stood for a moment on the porch looking up at the sky. He was a broad, bandy-legged little man with a walrus mustache, with square hands, puffed and muscled on the palms. His eyes were a contemplative, watery grey and the hair which protruded from under his Stetson hat was spiky and weathered. Billy was still stuffing his shirt into his blue jeans as he stood on the porch. He unbuckled his belt and tightened it again. The belt showed, by the worn shiny places opposite each hole, the gradual increase of Billy's middle over a period of years. When he had seen to the weather, Billy cleared each nostril by holding its mate closed with his forefinger and blowing fiercely. Then he walked down to the barn, rubbing his hands together. He curried and brushed two saddle horses in the stalls, talking quietly to them all the time; and he had hardly finished when the iron triangle started ringing at the ranch house.

Do we like—or dislike—this character? We don't know yet, but we certainly *see* him.

This is the opening of John Le Carré's 1986 novel, *A Perfect Spy*:

> In the small hours of a blustery October morning in a south Devon coastal town that seemed to have been deserted by its inhabitants, Magnus Pym got out of his elderly country

taxi-cab and, having paid the driver and waited till he had left, struck out across the church square. His destination was a terrace of ill-lit Victorian boarding-houses with names like Bel-a-Vista, The Commodore and Eureka. In build he was powerful but stately, a representative of something. His stride was agile, his body forward-sloping in the best tradition of the Anglo-Saxon administrative class. In the same attitude, whether static

> "Do we like—or dislike—this character? We don't know yet, but we certainly see him."

or in motion, Englishmen have hoisted flags over distant colonies, discovered the sources of great rivers, stood on the decks of sinking ships. He had been travelling in one way or another for sixteen hours but he wore no overcoat or hat. He carried a fat black briefcase of the official kind and in the other hand a green Harrods bag. A strong sea wind lashed at his city suit, salt rain stung his eyes, balls of spume skimmed across his path. Pym ignored them. Reaching the porch of a house marked "No Vacancies" he pressed the bell and waited, first for the outside light to go on, then for the chains to be unfastened from inside. While he waited a church clock began striking five. As if in answer to its summons Pym turned on his heel and stared back at the square. At the graceless tower of the Baptist church posturing against the racing clouds. At the writhing monkey-puzzle trees, pride of the ornamental gardens. At the empty bandstand. At the bus shelter. At the dark patches of the side streets. At the doorways one by one.

"Why Mr. Canterbury, it's you," an old lady's voice objected sharply as the door opened behind him. "You bad man. You caught the night sleeper again, I can tell. Why ever didn't you telephone?"

"Hullo, Miss Dubber," said Pym. "How are you?"

"Never mind how I am, Mr. Canterbury. Come in at once. You'll catch your death."

But the ugly windswept square seemed to have locked Pym in its spell. "I thought Sea View was up for sale, Miss D," he remarked as she tried to pluck him into the house. "You told me Mr. Cook moved out when his wife died. Wouldn't set foot in the place, you said."

"Of course he wouldn't. He was allergic. Come in this instant, Mr. Canterbury, and wipe your feet before I make your tea."

"So what's a light doing in his upstairs bedroom window?" Pym asked as he allowed her to tug him up the steps.

Like many tyrants Miss Dubber was small. She was also old and powdery and lopsided, with a crooked back that rumpled her dressing-gown and made everything round her seem lopsided too.

"Mr. Cook has rented out the upper flat, Celia Venn has taken it to paint in. That's you all over." She slid a bolt. "Disappear for three months, come back in the middle of the night and worry about a light in someone's window." She slid another. "You'll never change, Mr. Canterbury. I don't know why I bother."

"Who on earth is Celia Venn?"

"Dr. Venn's daughter, silly. She wants to see the sea and paint it." Her voice changed abruptly. "Why Mr. Canterbury, how dare you? Take that off this instant."

With the last bolt in place Miss Dubber had straightened up as best she could and was preparing herself for a reluctant hug. But instead of her customary scowl, which nobody believed in for a moment, her poky little face had twisted in fright.

"Your horrid black tie, Mr. Canterbury. I won't have death in the house, I won't have you bring it. Who is it for?"

Pym was a handsome man, boyish but distinguished. In his early fifties he was in his prime, full of zeal and urgency in a place that knew none. But the best thing about him in Miss Dubber's view was his lovely smile that gave out so much warmth and truth and made her feel right.

So, here in a small number of words, we have two good vivid characterizations, one obviously a major character, probably *the* major character, and another, clearly a minor one. Plus we have a bonus—an intriguing plot device:

The two seemed to know each other well and for some time. There's only one thing—Miss Dubber doesn't know Mr. Canterbury's real name. Why?

80 ❖ CR

Hemingway began his famous novel, *The Sun Also Rises*, with a description of a character but, oddly enough, not of his protagonist nor the heroine of the book:

> Robert Cohn was once middleweight boxing champion of Princeton. Do not think that I am very much impressed by that as a boxing title, but it meant a lot to Cohn. He cared nothing for boxing, in fact he disliked it, but he learned it painfully and thoroughly to counteract the feeling of inferiority and shyness he had felt on being treated as a Jew at Princeton. There was a certain inner comfort in knowing he could knock down anybody who was snooty to him, although, being very shy and a thoroughly nice boy, he never fought except in the gym. He was Spider Kelly's star pupil. Spider Kelly taught all his young gentlemen to box like featherweights, no matter whether they weighed one hundred and five or two hundred and five pounds. But it seemed to fit Cohn. He was really very fast. He was so good that Spider promptly overmatched him and got his nose permanently flattened. This increased Cohn's distaste for boxing, but it gave him a certain satisfaction of some strange sort, and it certainly improved his nose. In his last year at Princeton he read too much and took to wearing spectacles. I never met any one of his class who remembered him. They did not even remember that he was middleweight boxing champion.

Where is Hemingway going with this? Is it a story about a boxer? Not at all. But we read on:

> I mistrust all frank and simple people, especially when their stories hold together, and I always had a suspicion that perhaps Robert Cohn had never been middleweight boxing champion, and that perhaps a horse had stepped on his face, or that maybe

his mother had been frightened or seen something, or that he had, maybe, bumped into something as a young child, but I finally had somebody verify the story from Spider Kelly. Spider Kelly not only remembered Cohn. He had often wondered what had become of him.

Robert Cohn was a member, through his father, of one of the richest Jewish families in New York, and through his mother of one of the oldest. At the military school where he prepped for Princeton, and played a very good end on the football team, no one had made him race-conscious. No one had ever made him feel he was a Jew, and hence any different from anybody else, until he went to Princeton. He was a nice boy, a friendly boy, and very shy, and it made him bitter. He took it out in boxing, and he came out of Princeton with painful self-consciousness and the flattened nose, and was married by the first girl who was nice to him. He was married five years, had three children, lost most of the fifty thousand dollars his father left him, the balance of the estate having gone to his mother, hardened into a rather unattractive mould under domestic unhappiness with a rich wife, and just when he had made up his mind to leave his wife she left him and went off with a miniature-painter. As he had been thinking for months about leaving his wife and had not done it because it would be too cruel to deprive her of himself, her departure was a very healthful shock.

Cohn is a secondary character in the story but takes on more importance in the last third. Jake Barnes, whose World War I wound has rendered him impotent, is now a newspaperman in Paris who is futilely in love with Lady Brett Ashley, a high-living, high-loving English divorcée. When Jake and his hard-drinking cronies decide to go to Spain for the running of the bulls, Brett and her British fiancé, a charming drunkard, join them. Robert Cohn, desperately and pathetically in love with the promiscuous Lady Brett, boorishly intrudes on the group. During the drunken week she has an affair with the handsome bullfighter who Cohn promptly beats up and then, full of remorse, disappears from the story altogether. Lady Brett runs off with the matador but soon breaks up with him and runs to her friend Jake for consolation.

Early in the novel's beginning, Hemingway lets the reader know the central problem—that Jake is impotent. In the end the author reminds us of that conflict, even to the subtle reference to the policeman's baton.

In Madrid, after a dinner (involving three martinis apiece, plus three bottles of wine!) this scene takes place in a taxi:

> We sat close against each other. I put my arm around her and she rested against me comfortably. It was very hot and bright, and the houses looked sharply white. We turned out onto the Gran Via.
>
> "Oh, Jake," Brett said, "we could have had such a damned good time together."
>
> Ahead was a mounted policeman in khaki directing traffic. He raised his baton. The car slowed suddenly pressing Brett against me.
>
> "Yes," I said. "Isn't it pretty to think so?"

A good and justly famous ending that justifies the beginning.

✔ When *The Sun Also Rises* was published in 1924, the reviews were ecstatic, especially about Hemingway's style and dialogue.

"The dialogue is brilliant. It is alive with the rhythms and idioms, the pauses and suspensions and innuendoes and shorthands, of living speech. It is in the dialogue, almost entirely, that Mr. Hemingway tells his story and makes the people live and act."

—Conrad Aiken, *New York Herald Tribune*

As Elmore Leonard told the students at the 2000 Santa Barbara Writers Conference:
"You can do it all with dialogue."

℘ ❖ ℃

Starting a short story with a physical description of a character has never gone out of fashion.

In her story "Luda and Milena," published in the *New Yorker*, September 2007, here's how the author, Lara Vapynyar, begins:

Milena had large blue eyes, an elegant nose, and olive skin covered with a graceful network of fine wrinkles. "Her face is a battlefield for anti-aging creams," Luda said of Milena, adding that she wouldn't want youth that came from bottles and jars. Once, Luda brought old photographs of herself to class to show Milena that she, too, had been a real beauty. The photographs revealed an attractive woman with a sturdy hourglass figure, imposing dense brows, and very dark eyes. Some people saw a striking resemblance to the young Elizabeth Taylor, but Milena didn't. Milena said that the young Luda looked like Saddam Hussein with bigger hair and a thinner mustache.

> ❝ Starting a short story with a physical description of a character has never gone out of fashion. ❞

The two women met on the first day of a free E.S.L. class held in one of the musty back rooms of Brooklyn College. Luda was late. She had been babysitting her two grandchildren, and her son-in-law had failed to come home on time. Angry and flustered, Luda had had to run all the way to the college, pushing through the rush-hour subway crowd, cutting through the meat market on Nostrand Avenue, and having the following exchange with a large woman in a pink jacket:

WOMAN: "Watch it, asshole!"

LUDA: "No, it is you asshole!"

℘ ❖ ℃

Comparing one's characters to a well-known actor or a public figure or an historical figure is a tried and true gimmick, perhaps too tried, too lazy, too easy, viz.: "so handsome he made Clark Gable look like Ernest Borgnine."

William Styron, in his huge bestseller *Sophie's Choice*, has the drunken, evil S.S. doctor choose between which of her children is to die—as looking "a bit like a militarized Leslie Howard, whom she had had a mild crush on ever since *The Petrified Forest*."

If one is going to do this, be sure it doesn't come out anachronistic; for example, it might be all right to state that Abraham Lincoln looked like Julius Caesar but not that Julius Caesar looked like Abraham Lincoln.

My favorite reference of this sort of literary flourish is James Thurber's description of his erstwhile boss, Harold Ross, founder of the *New Yorker* magazine: "He looked like a dishonest Abraham Lincoln."

The beginning of Paul Theroux's 1996 novel *My Other Life* consists of a long, very long, description of Hal, an outrageously eccentric uncle of the narrator, which begins like this:

> When people say of someone, "You'll either love him or hate him," I always have the feeling I'll hate him. Then I remember my Uncle Hal and I know better.
>
> Uncle Hal seldom spoke to us except to tease or criticize, but once he told me that his mother—Grandma—had never picked him up when he cried in his crib. She simply let him lie there and scream—didn't touch him, didn't talk to him, didn't feed him until a specific minute on the clock. He must have been forty-something when he confided this, and he looked at me and added, "Imagine what that can do to a person, Paulie."
>
> He was unshaven and his whiskers were grayer than they should have been. He was always clawing his hair. I never saw him sit down at his table to eat a meal. He stood up, looking out of the kitchen window, forking tuna fish out of an open can, then he threw the can away and wiped his hands on his shirt. He drank out of bottles—even milk bottles, even milk cartons that had spouts that missed his lips. He put his mouth under the faucet. He hated the way that other people ate—sitting down, taking their time. Just a small amount of sitting down made him jump up and rage. "We're wasting time! I've got so much to do! I've been sitting down all day!"
>
> His house needed painting, he said; his grass had to be cut. He needed something at the hardware store—and it might be a hinge that he would fasten by banging screws through the

holes as though they were nails, he was so impatient to get the thing hung. And the way he used a hammer made you think of a murderer.

"I'm going off-Cape," he would say, whether his destination was Boston to the dentist's or to Mexico, where he claimed he hunted giant lizards.

The description goes on for twelve pages! No real conflict, no promise of a story, just a detailed description—albeit a fascinating one—of this eccentric man.

Not a recommended formula for a beginning writer, unless you have as unique a character as Hal, or can write as skillfully as Paul Theroux.

ഔ ❖ ര

Elmore Leonard warns against physical descriptions that are too long and detailed, saying:

In Ernest Hemingway's "Hills Like White Elephants," what do the "American and the girl with him" look like? "She had taken off her hat and put it on the table." That's the only reference to a physical description in the story, and yet we see the couple and know them by their tones of voice, and not one adverb in sight.

Somerset Maugham says that it is quite enough if the reader knows whether his characters are good looking or not, and nice or not nice (but he seldom followed his own advice in his stories!).

In *Sweet Thursday*, John Steinbeck has a character say:

I like a lot of talk in a book and I don't like to have nobody tell me what the guy that's talking looks like. I want to figure out what he looks like from the way he talks...figure out what the guy's thinking from what he says. I like some description but not too much of that.

That's fine, but the average reader wants at least a few hints about the age and appearance of the principal characters.

Instead of the author *directly* describing a character, some writers elect to see the protagonist indirectly through the viewpoint of another character or characters. It is a tried-and-true method, used forever by playwrights especially. The curtain goes up, the butler and the maid are cleaning the living room—" 'ave ya noticed the missus is especially lovely now since she met that handsome, young painter chap?" etc. etc.

One of the first great indirect descriptions comes from Homer's *Iliad*. The Trojan War has dragged on for almost a decade and the Greek soldiers are complaining, fed up and wanting to go home, and wondering why they are fighting for some woman they haven't even seen—

—and then! Gorgeous Helen walks by. "Wow!" they say, in so many words, and they grab up their weapons and go back eagerly to the fray. We now truly believe Helen was beautiful and worth fighting for. The author didn't *tell* us—we *saw* the effect she and her beauty had on some battle-weary men.

International thriller writer Len Deighton chose to indirectly introduce the eponymous hero of his 1987 novel, *Winter*, through the eyes of an Austrian crowd, beginning his novel like this:

> Everyone saw the imperious man standing under the lamppost in Vienna's Ringstrasse, and yet no one looked directly at him. He was very slim, about thirty years old, pale-faced, with quick angry eyes and a neatly trimmed black mustache. His eyes were shadowed by the brim of his shiny silk top hat, and the gaslight picked out the diamond pin in his cravat. He wore a long black chesterfield overcoat with a fur collar. It was an especially fine-looking coat, the sort of overcoat that came from the exclusive tailors of Berlin. "I can't wait a moment longer," he said. And his German was spoken with the accent of Berlin. No one—except perhaps some of the immigrants from the Sudetenland who now made up such a large proportion of the city's population—could have mistaken Harald Winter for a native of Vienna.

Why did no one look directly at this man? That one small fact slipped in there will make the reader want more!

> Sometimes a simple statement will *insist* that we read on—like Stephen Crane's opening of his classic short story "The Open Boat" (which H.G. Wells called "The finest short story in the English language").
>
> "None of them knew the color of the sky."
>
> "Why?" the reader asks—and reads on!

You might think that Emily Brontë would begin her classic novel *Wuthering Heights* (1847) with a lush, adjective-laden valentine to her beloved moors which play such an important part in the background of the torrid love story between her protagonists, Cathy and Heathcliff.

But! She is too fine a storyteller not to want to get things moving right away, to introduce her pivotal character, and to let us know we're in for a strange and wild experience:

> I have just returned from a visit to my landlord—the solitary neighbour that I shall be troubled with. This is certainly a beautiful country! In all England, I do not believe that I could have fixed on a situation so completely removed from the stir of society. A perfect misanthropist's heaven; and Mr. Heathcliff and I are such a suitable pair to divide the desolation between us. A capital fellow! He little imagined how my heart warmed towards him when I beheld his black eyes withdraw so suspiciously under their brows, as I rode up, and when his fingers sheltered themselves, with a jealous resolution, still further in his waistcoat, as I announced my name.
>
> "Mr. Heathcliff!" I said.
>
> A nod was the answer.

A capital fellow?

This splendid opening is worth several readings, containing as it does so much information, subtle characterization, and hints of conflict to come. There is a nod to the setting—mercifully brief—("beautiful country!"— "so removed"—"desolation"), but it is the sly description of the "solitary neighbour" that engages the attention of Brontë—and her reader ("misanthropist's heaven"—"black eyes withdraw so suspiciously under their brows"—"fingers sheltered themselves"—"jealous resolution").

This guy Heathcliff is a man to approach with caution, and not for a moment do we subscribe to the naïve narrator's pronouncement that he is a "capital fellow."

And did you happen to notice that eighteenth word tossed off so casually—un-casually actually—in the first sentence?

TROUBLED!

Stories are about *trouble*—or more probably—*troubles* with a capital *T*. The troubles are either solved or not, but it is why we read stories—we read to see how characters react and cope with their *troubles*, overcoming or succumbing to them.

2

Setting

In the old days, before tv and movies, when people had more time to read, writers would start their stories with descriptions, often long ones, of where the coming story was to take place. And weather—lots of weather, always.

"It was a dark and stormy night" is not a bad opening sentence. It is the opening of *Paul Clifford*, a novel by the first Earl of Lytton, a dedicated whist player and author of several popular Victorian novels. If only he had not gone on after that first sentence! Unfortunately, he followed it with this turgid sentence:

> The rain fell in torrents, except at occasional intervals, when it was checked by a violent gust of wind which swept up the streets (for it is in London that our scene lies), rattling along the housetops, and fiercely agitating the scanty flame of the lamps that struggled against the darkness.

—and thus the Earl of Lytton achieved a sort of literary infamy, perpetuated by many, including Charles Schulz's dog Snoopy who, when at the typewriter, began almost every story with "It was a dark and stormy night," or a variation of that sentence. ("It was a sort of dark and sort of stormy night," etc.)

The *New Yorker* magazine writer Donald Barthelme, in his writing workshops, used to pound the table and declare: "Students, no weather, *please!*"

Barthelme surely must have been impatient with—if not aghast at— Charles Dickens' beginning of *Bleak House*. Though considered one of the great writer's best novels and written at age forty when Dickens was at the height of his powers, he starts out with no characters—just fog, page after page of fog.

Try reading Dickens' opening. Be honest: If you were to pick this book up today thinking it a current novel and without knowing it was a classic by one of the world's greatest novelists, would you continue reading? (Feel free to stop reading at any time.)

London. Michaelmas term lately over, and the Lord Chancellor sitting in Lincoln's Inn Hall. Implacable November weather. As much mud in the streets as if the waters had but newly retired from the face of the earth, and it would not be wonderful to meet a Megalosaurus, forty feet long or so, waddling like an elephantine lizard up Holborn Hill. Smoke lowering down from chimney-pots, making a soft black drizzle, with flakes of soot in it as big as full-grown snowflakes—gone into mourning, one might imagine, for the death of the sun. Dogs, undistinguishable in mire. Horses, scarcely better; splashed to their very blinkers. Foot passengers, jostling one another's umbrellas in a general infection of ill temper, and losing their foothold at street-corners, where tens of thousands of other foot passengers have been slipping and sliding since the day broke (if this day ever broke), adding new deposits to the crust upon crust of mud, sticking at those points tenaciously to the pavement, and accumulating at compound interest.

Fog everywhere. Fog up the river, where it flows among green aits and meadows; fog down the river, where it rolls defiled among the tiers of shipping and the waterside pollutions of a great (and dirty) city. Fog on the Essex marshes, fog on the Kentish heights. Fog creeping into the cabooses of collier-brigs; fog lying out on the yards and hovering in the rigging of great ships; fog drooping on the gunwales of barges and small boats. Fog in the eyes and throats of ancient Greenwich pensioners, wheezing by the firesides of their wards; fog in the stem and bowl of the afternoon pipe of the wrathful skipper, down in his close cabin; fog cruelly pinching the toes and fingers of his shivering little 'prentice boy on deck. Chance people on the bridges peeping over the parapets into a nether sky of fog, with fog all round them, as if they were up in a balloon and hanging in the misty clouds.

Gas looming through the fog in divers places in the streets, much as the sun may, from the spongey fields, be seen to loom by husbandman and ploughboy. Most of the shops lighted two hours before their time—as the gas seems to know, for it has a haggard and unwilling look.

The raw afternoon is rawest, and the dense fog is densest, and the muddy streets are muddiest near that leaden-headed old obstruction, appropriate ornament for the threshold of a leaden-headed old corporation, Temple Bar. And hard by Temple Bar, in Lincoln's Inn Hall, at the very heart of the fog, sits the Lord High Chancellor in his High Court of Chancery.

Never can there come fog too thick, never can there come mud and mire too deep, to assort with the groping and floundering condition which this High Court of Chancery, most pestilent of hoary sinners, holds this day in the sight of heaven and earth.

At last we get to a human being. Dare we hope for a *story?*

On such an afternoon, if ever, the Lord High Chancellor ought to be sitting here—as here he is—with a foggy glory round his head, softly fenced in with crimson cloth and curtains, addressed by a large advocate with great whiskers, a little voice, and an interminable brief, and outwardly directing his contemplation to the lantern in the roof, where he can see nothing but fog. On such an afternoon....

> " At last we get to a human being. Dare we hope for a *story?* "

—and Dickens *finally* gets to his story, though he's not entirely through with his fog. He's besotted by fog, poor bloke.

This beautifully written piece becomes tedious because the reader, in quest of a story, demands a living creature—man, woman, or animal—in the center of a setting. In today's writing world, should the writer ignore setting and weather? Of course not.

How would one of today's writers of best-selling thrillers have started the novel and still established the setting and weather? Perhaps something like this:

> When he ran out of his London townhouse to look for her, the thick fog—the thickest he'd ever encountered—the cursed fog enveloped him so that he could barely see. Where in God's name was she?

What Dickens gave us in a heavy dose was *inert material.*

What is *inert material?* Here is what A.B. Guthrie, author of such exciting novels as *The Big Sky* (and the screenplay for the film *Shane*), says about it in his little book *A Field Guide to Writing Fiction:*

> Anything off the story line constitutes what can be called inert material.
>
> Exposition, explanation, description independent of your running narrative is inert. There it lies, an obstacle to the run of your story, a dam in the current.
>
> And it is so easy to forget or ignore the simple fact that description of an object or process must be integrated with the story's movement.

An inert passage doesn't go anywhere. It exists all by itself, remote from character and action. It is off-scene or, as Hollywood says, "off-camera." Take Melville's *Moby Dick.* Here is page after page of exposition in the middle of the story as the author speaks at length of the ship and its components and the whaling industry in general. The story comes to a halt for a while. To be sure, all this imparted knowledge comes in useful later on, but nevertheless it lies dead in the living story. It is as if Melville had taken time off from fiction to explain about a ship, an industry, and its workings. He may be excused by the fact that in the 1840s there was no *National Geographic* or TV or Wikipedia, and few people knew anything about the whaling industry. He is preparing the reader for what is to come and being tedious in the process, but, of course, the novel survives because of the iconic story that has been set in motion by a good beginning.

If you choose to begin your story with inert material, by describing weather or scenery or by, say, taking inventory of a parlor, you must write very well if you are to engage the attention of the reader.

છ ❖ ૭

Here is the masterful opening by F. Scott Fitzgerald of his 1933 novel *Tender Is the Night* which begins, normally fatally, with pure description:

> On the pleasant shore of the French Riviera, about half way between Marseilles and the Italian border, stands a large, proud, rose-colored hotel. Deferential palms cool its flushed façade, and before it stretches a short dazzling beach. Lately it has become a summer resort of notable and fashionable people; a decade ago it was almost deserted after its English clientele went north in April. Now, many bungalows cluster near it, but when this story begins only the cupolas of a dozen old villas rotted like water lilies among the massed pines between Gausse's Hôtel des Étrangers and Cannes, five miles away.
>
> The hotel and its bright tan prayer rug of a beach were one. In the early morning the distant images of Cannes, the pink and cream of old fortifications, the purple Alp that bounded Italy, were cast across the water and lay quavering in the ripples and rings sent up by sea-plants through the clear shallows. Before eight a man came down to the beach in a blue bathrobe and with much preliminary application to his person of the chilly water, and much grunting and loud breathing, floundered a minute in the sea. When he had gone, beach and bay were quiet for an hour. Merchantmen crawled westward on the horizon; bus boys shouted in the hotel court; the dew dried upon the pines. In another hour the horns of motors began to blow down from the winding road along the low range of the Maures, which separates the littoral from true Provençal France.

I would have started the story with the following, *then* gone back to the setting. But then, Scott didn't ask for my opinion.

A mile from the sea, where pines give way to dusty poplars, is an isolated railroad stop, whence one June morning in 1925 a Victoria brought a woman and her daughter down to Gausse's Hotel. The mother's face was of a fading prettiness that would soon be patted with broken veins; her expression was both tranquil and aware in a pleasant way. However, one's eye moved on quickly to her daughter, who had magic in her pink palms and her cheeks lit to a lovely flame, like the thrilling flush of children after their cold baths in the evening. Her fine forehead sloped gently up to where her hair, bordering it like an armorial shield, burst into lovelocks and waves and curlicues of ash blonde and gold. Her eyes were bright, big, clear, wet, and shining, the color of her cheeks was real, breaking close to the surface from the strong young pump of her heart. Her body hovered delicately on the last edge of childhood—she was almost eighteen, nearly complete, but the dew was still on her.

As sea and sky appeared below them in a thin, hot line the mother said:

"Something tells me we're not going to like this place."

Fitzgerald certainly puts us immediately in the colorful south of France, but did we pick up this book for a travelogue?

Although the first two paragraphs are static ones, notice how quickly the author—*has something happening!*

But would it be soon enough in a story to satisfy today's editors?

In the third paragraph, on a specific day, two people are arriving. Something, however uneventful, is *happening*. They are two seemingly ordinary characters but they are intriguingly described.

Then, very soon, we get the artful and seducing line of *foreshadowing*: "Something tells me we're not going to like this place."

Then, we sit up and pay more attention.

And, notice in this uneventful but splendid beginning Fitzgerald's lack of clichés and his vigorous verbs that give life to what could be dull description: *cool, cluster, rotted, quavering, floundered, crawled, dried, patted.*

As most professional writers urge: "Forget the adverb; get the *right* and *vigorous* verb!"

ᛋᏅ ❖ ᏣᏚ

One of John Steinbeck's most memorable stories, "The Ears of Johnny Bear," an astonishing story with a shocking ending, starts very placidly with a plain description of a small California town:

> The village of Loma is built, as its name implies, on a low, round hill that rises like an island out of the flat mouth of the Salinas Valley in central California. To the north and east of the town a black tule swamp stretches for miles, but to the south the marsh has been drained. Rich vegetable land has been the result of the draining, land so black with wealth that the lettuce and cauliflowers grow to giants.
>
> The owners of the swamp to the north of the village grew covetous of the black land. They banded together and formed a reclamation district. I work for the company which took the contract to put a ditch through. The floating clam-shell digger arrived, was put together and started eating a ditch of open water through the swamp.
>
> I tried living in the floating bunkhouse with the crew for a while, but the mosquitoes that hung in banks over the dredger and the heavy pestilential mist that sneaked out of the swamp every night and slid near to the ground drove me into the village of Loma, where I took a furnished room, the most dismal I have ever seen, in the house of Mrs. Ratz. I might have looked farther, but the idea of having my mail come in care of Mrs. Ratz decided me. After all I only slept in the bare, cold room. I ate my meals in the galley of the floating bunkhouse.
>
> There aren't more than two hundred people in Loma. The Methodist church has the highest place on the hill; its spire is visible for miles. Two groceries, a hardware store, an ancient Masonic Hall and the Buffalo Bar comprise the public

> "As most professional writers urge: Forget the adverb; get the *right* and *vigorous* verb!"

buildings. On the side of the hills are the small wooden houses of the population, and on the rich southern flats are the houses of the landowners, small yards usually enclosed by high walls of clipped cypress to keep out the driving afternoon winds.

There was nothing to do in Loma in the evening except to go to the saloon, an old board building with swinging doors and a wooden sidewalk awning. Neither prohibition nor repeal had changed its business, its clientele nor the quality of its whiskey. In the course of an evening every male inhabitant of Loma over fifteen years old came at least once to the Buffalo Bar, had a drink, talked a while and went home.

Okay, okay—Steinbeck goes on more about this quiet town and while it is a fine picture of a boring place, it is—well, boring. We are not grabbed; if the reader didn't know that the author was John Steinbeck, he might not continue reading; from John Steinbeck we want great characters and things happening!

Then all of a sudden the story begins:

I was sitting in the bar one night talking to Alex Hartnell who owned a nice little farm. We were talking about black bass fishing, when the front doors opened and swung closed. A hush fell on the men in the room. Alex nudged me and said, "It's Johnny Bear." I looked around.

His name described him better than I can. He looked like a great, stupid, smiling bear. His black matted head bobbed forward and his long arms hung out as though he should have been on all fours and was only standing upright as a trick. His legs were short and bowed, ending with strange, square feet. He was dressed in dark blue denim, but his feet were bare; they didn't seem to be crippled or deformed in any way, but they were square, just as wide as they were long. He stood in the doorway, swinging his arms jerkily the way halfwits do. On his face there was a foolish happy smile. He moved forward and for all his bulk and clumsiness, he seemed to creep. He didn't move like a man, but like some prowling night animal. At the bar he stopped, his little bright eyes went about from face to face expectantly, and he asked, "Whiskey?"

Loma was not a treating town. A man might buy a drink
for another if he were pretty sure the other would immediately
buy one for him. I was surprised when one of the quiet men
laid a coin on the counter. Fat Carl filled the glass. The monster
took it and gulped the whiskey.

"What the devil—" I began. But Alex nudged me and
said "Sh."

And what a story it is.

Johnny Bear is retarded, to say the least, but he is a human recording
machine; he is a peeping tom, going from house to house, and, without
understanding what he is hearing, the conversations are implanted word
for word, no matter in what language, in Johnny's brain. He then goes to
the Buffalo Bar to recite his previous night's eavesdropping verbatim in
exchange for a shot or two of whiskey.

The basic story revolves around the Hawkins' sisters, wealthy un-
married ladies. They are beloved and respected by the townspeople who
consider them their aristocrats. When Miss Amy, the younger of the two,
hangs herself, the town is shocked. And they are even more shocked when
they learn she was pregnant. They learn it from Johnny Bear who repeats
a conversation he eavesdropped between the sister and the town doctor.
And then the real shocker is when Johnny Bear repeats a conversation
in Chinese between Miss Amy and the Chinese field hand who we learn
was—her lover!

So it is a good story—so how do I dare say to the great John Steinbeck
that its beginning is not memorable? Perhaps in the many, many years
since he wrote the story there have been so many competitive writers
saying, "Hey, read me, read me. I'm the story you need to read…and
buy! Or to hell with it, go watch television!"

One way that Steinbeck could have had a more interesting beginning
and still have lost none of his good depiction of the town would have been
to put the narrator into the story at the very beginning, viz.:

"It was payday, and I'd borrowed a horse to ride into town.
I knew my buddies would be at the Buffalo Bar and I didn't want
to miss the action because, without that bar, my life in Loma
was a pretty lonely one. Come to think of it, a lot of folks lead
lonely lives here, and lonely people can be plenty nosy.

"The horse, an old gelding with gaunt withers, snorted as we passed by the swamp on the north side of town..."

Et cetera, as we get an impression of Loma from *a person* instead of from the author.

℘ ❖ ℭ

When Elmore Leonard spoke to the Santa Barbara Writers Conference some years ago, he was asked:

"Mr. Leonard, how do you generate such suspense in your writing?"

He answered simply and wonderfully:

"I try to leave out all the parts that readers skip."

What would Mr. Leonard think of *Birdsong*, a novel published in 1993 by Sebastian Faulkes? It is a splendid book but it begins in an old-fashioned, sorry, boring way:

The boulevard du Cange was a broad, quiet street that marked the eastern flank of the city of Amiens. The wagons that rolled in from Lille and Arras to the north drove directly into the tanneries and mills of the Saint Leu quarter without needing to use this rutted, leafy road. The town side of the boulevard backed on to substantial gardens, which were squared off and apportioned with civic precision to the houses they adjoined. On the damp grass were chestnut trees, lilacs, and willows, cultivated to give shade and quietness to their owners. The gardens had a wild, overgrown look and their deep lawns and bursting hedges could conceal small clearings, quiet pools, and areas unvisited even by the inhabitants, where patches of grass and wild flowers lay beneath the branches of overhanging trees.

Z-z-z-z? Yes—but Faulkes keeps going on and on with more setting. I skip ahead and am about to give up and watch *Jeopardy*, but suddenly there's a mention of—*Humans*!

Wow!

It's just a house, but I'll take it. I'll take it because houses often contain humans! Consider the following:

> The Azaires' house showed a strong, formal front toward the road from behind iron railings. The traffic looping down to the river would have been in no doubt that this was the property of a substantial man. The slate roof plunged in conflicting angles to cover the irregular shape of the house. Beneath one of them a dormer window looked out on to the boulevard. The first floor was dominated by a stone balcony, over whose balustrades the red ivy had crept on its way up to the roof. There was a formidable front door with iron facings on the timber.
>
> Inside, the house was both smaller and larger than it looked. It had no rooms of intimidating grandeur, no gilt ballrooms with dripping chandeliers, yet it had unexpected spaces and corridors that disclosed new corners with steps down into the gardens; there were small salons equipped with writing desks and tapestry-covered chairs that opened inward from unregarded passageways. Even from the end of the lawn, it was difficult to see how the rooms and corridors were fitted into the placid rectangles of stone. Throughout the building the floors made distinctive sounds beneath the press of feet, so that with its closed angles and echoing air, the house was always a place of unseen footsteps.
>
> Stephen Wraysford's metal trunk had been sent ahead and was waiting at the foot of the bed.

At last we have a character to focus on—well, okay, at least his trunk.

> He unpacked his clothes and hung his spare suit in the giant carved wardrobe. There was an enamel wash bowl and wooden towel rail beneath the window. He had to stand on tiptoe to look out over the boulevard, where a cab was waiting on the other side of the street, the horse shaking its harness and

reaching up its neck to nibble at the branches of a lime tree. He tested the resilience of the bed, then lay down on it, resting his head on the concealed bolster. The room was simple but had been decorated with some care. There was a vase of wild flowers on the table and two prints of street scenes in Honfleur on either side of the door.

It was a spring evening, with a late sun in the sky beyond the cathedral and the sound of blackbirds from either side of the house. Stephen washed perfunctorily and tried to flatten his black hair in the small mirror. He placed half a dozen cigarettes in a metal case that he tucked inside his jacket. He emptied his pockets of items he no longer needed: railway tickets, a blue leather notebook, and a knife with a single, scrupulously sharpened blade.

Considering that this truly great novel is romantic, erotic and at times, violent, this tame beginning is surprisingly mild, and the sad thing is that many readers, like me, might have given up on it because of the first pages!

80 ❖ ଔ

Just for fun, go to your local bookstore tomorrow. They usually have a table featuring the best-selling novels. Turn over the cover of each, go to the first page, and see how many start with pure setting and no characters.

It can be done, it has been done, and it will be done—but writing fiction is difficult enough. Why make it harder to engage the reader?

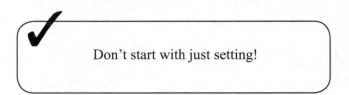

Don't start with just setting!

3

Setting—Plus a Character

RATHER THAN MERELY DESCRIBING A SETTING AND THE WEATHER, a more modern and intriguing way to begin a story or novel is to incorporate your protagonist—or antagonist—in the midst of his or her setting.

For example, which of these two beginning sentences would attract your interest the most?

At dusk the rain was coming down in sheets on crowded Fifth Avenue.

or:

As Melanie fled down crowded Fifth Avenue at exactly 5:36 in the afternoon, the heavy rain pelted her face and mingled with her tears.

In the second example we have sacrificed none of the description of the first, plus we have a character and the beginning of a story to pique our interest. Why is she fleeing, and why is she crying? And why is the exact time important?

Conflict!

Plus, we have included just enough setting and weather for us to *see* where the happening is taking place.

Instead of breaking out a lot of adjectives and describing the little cabin in the sunset at the base of the hill, how about seeing it from a character's point of view:

At the base of the hill, Gene turned in the saddle for a moment and looked back at the cabin, gilded now by the setting sun, and by the fire he'd just set in the kerosene-soaked bed.

ℬ ❖ ℭ

Donald Barthelme, who so adamantly decreed "no weather!", might be astonished to read a recent short story by fellow *New Yorker* writer, the famous John Updike ("Outage," January 7, 2008). It begins with— horror!—*weather*!

The weatherpersons on television, always eager for ratings-boosting disasters, had predicted a fierce autumn storm for New England, with driving rain and high winds.

But Updike is too accomplished a writer to focus on just weather alone for long. His next sentence immediately gets to the nitty-gritty; how is the weather—this particular weather—going to affect his protagonist?

Brad Morris who worked at home while his wife, Jane, managed a boutique on Boston's Newbury Street, glanced out his windows now and then at the swaying trees—oaks still tenacious of their rusty leaves, maples letting go in gusts of gold and red—but was unimpressed by the hyped news event. Rains came down heavily a half hour at a time, then pulled back into a silvery sky of fast-moving, fuzzy-bottomed clouds. The worst seemed to be over, when, in midafternoon, his computer died under his eyes. The financial figures he had been painstakingly assembling swooned as a group, sucked into the dead blank screen like glittering water pulled down a drain. Around him, the house seemed to sigh, as all its lights and little engines, its computerized timers and indicators, simultaneously shut down. The sound of wind and rain lashing the trees outside infiltrated the silence. A beam creaked. A loose shutter banged. The drip from a plugged gutter tapped heavily, like a bully nagging for attention, on the wooden cover of a cellar-window well.

We not only forgive Updike for starting with the weather but we admire him—because in this story, as in Jack London's "To Build a Fire," one of the finest stories ever written, "the weather" turns out to be not just window dressing but the protagonist, antagonist, and the *deus ex machina*; the weather *causes* the story.

ℰ ❖ ℛ

We need, of course, to know where a story is taking place and if it's terribly hot or cold, et cetera, but if something is *happening* in that setting or if we are introduced to a fascinating character we will become interested in reading on. Gone are the days when the author began his tale by describing a house or a meadow or a parlor in great tedious detail. Take Oscar Wilde's opening from his novel *The Picture of Dorian Gray*:

> The studio was filled with the rich odour of roses, and when the light summer wind stirred amidst the trees of the garden, there came through the open door the heavy scent of the lilac, or the more delicate perfume of the pink-flowering thorn.
>
> From the corner of the divan of Persian saddle-bags on which he was lying, smoking, as was his custom, innumerable cigarettes, Lord Henry Wotton could just catch the gleam of the honey-sweet and honey-coloured blossoms of a laburnum, whose tremulous branches seemed hardly able to bear the burden of a beauty so flame-like as theirs; and now and then the fantastic shadows of birds in flight flitted across the long tussore-silk curtains that were stretched in front of the huge window, producing a kind of momentary Japanese effect, and making him think of those pallid jade-faced painters of Tokio who, through the medium of an art that is necessarily immobile, seek to convey the sense of swiftness and motion. The sullen murmur of the bees shouldering their way through the long unmown grass, or circling with monotonous insistence round the dusty gilt horns of the straggling woodbine, seemed to make the stillness more oppressive. The dim roar of London was like the bourdon note of a distant organ.

Z-z-z-z-z-z------

Inert material!

The author does get to the story eventually, and a fine dramatic and classic story it is, but this sort of beginning would not please an editor—or reader—in today's world.

Contrast that genteel, and boring, beginning with this one by the modern writer of great international thrillers, Alan Furst. It is the start of his novel, *Night Soldiers*, published in 1989:

> In Bulgaria, in 1934, on a muddy street in the river town of Vidin, Khristo Stoianev saw his brother kicked to death by fascist militia.
>
> His brother was fifteen, no more than a blameless fool with a big mouth, and in calmer days his foolishness would have been accommodated in the usual ways—a slap in the face for humiliation, a few cold words to chill the blood, and a kick in the backside to send him on his way. That much was tradition. But these were *political* times, and it was very important to think before you spoke. Nikko Stoianev spoke without thinking, and so he died.
>
> On both sides of the river—Romania to the north and Bulgaria to the south—the political passion ran white hot. People talked of little else: in the marketplace, in the church, even—a mark of just how far matters had progressed—in the kitchen. *Something has happened in Bucharest. Something has happened in Sofia.*
>
> *Soon, something will happen here.*

There is no fancy description here, but we know where we are and what we are up against. We have a protagonist and victim, we have conflict, and we have a setting.

ഔ ❖ ଔ

James M. Cain practically invented the hardboiled novel and was a favorite writer of such disparate authors as Sinclair Lewis, Raymond Chandler, Ross Macdonald, and Mickey Spillane. He was famous for his fast, tough, and atmospheric beginnings, starting with his first novel, *The Postman Always Rings Twice* (1934), whose first sentence is:

They threw me off the haytruck about noon.

That doesn't seem like such a breakthrough today, but in those days people didn't start novels that way. They also didn't write openly about homosexuality, which lies at the core of his 1937 novel, *Serenade*. (Any suggestion of the "core" was surgically removed from the 1956 motion picture version starring Mario Lanza and Joan Fontaine.)

Here is how the novel begins:

> I was in the Tupinamba, having a *bizcocho* and coffee, when this girl came in. Everything about her said Indian, from the maroon *rebozo* to the black dress with purple flowers on it, to the swaying way she walked, that no woman ever got without carrying pots, bundles, and baskets on her head from the time she could crawl. But she wasn't any of the colors that Indians come in. She was almost white, with just the least dip of *café con leche*. Her shape was Indian, but not ugly. Most Indian women have a rope of muscle over their hips that give them a high-waisted, mis-shapen look, thin, bunchy legs, and too much breast-works. She had plenty in that line, but her hips were round, and her legs had a soft line to them. She was slim, but there was something voluptuous about her, like in three or four years she would get fat. All that, though, I only half saw. What I noticed was her face. It was flat, like an Indian's but the nose broke high, so it kind of went with the way she held her head, and the eyes weren't dumb, with that shiny, shoe-button look. They were pretty big, and black, but they leveled out straight, and had kind of a sleepy, impudent look to them. Her lips were thick, but pretty, and of course had plenty of lipstick on them.

Okay, Cain has introduced us to an interesting character; now he moves to a description of the place.

> It was about nine o'clock at night, and the place was pretty full, with bullfight managers, agents, newspaper men, pimps, cops and almost everybody you can think of, except somebody you would trust with your watch. She went to the bar and

ordered a drink, then went to a table and sat down, and I had a stifled feeling I had had before, from the thin air up there, but that wasn't it this time. There hadn't been any woman in my life for quite some while, and I knew what this meant. Her drink came, and it was coca-cola and Scotch, and I thought that over. It might mean that she was just starting the evening, and it might mean she was just working up an appetite, and if it meant that I was sunk. The Tupinamba is more of a café than a restaurant, but plenty of people eat there, and if that was what she expected to do, my last three pesos wouldn't go very far.

We learn a little about the narrator—he is broke. We like stories about people at the end of their rope.

I had about decided to take a chance and go over there when she moved. She slipped over to a place about two tables away, and then she moved again, and I saw what she was up to. She was closing in on a bullfighter named Triesca, a kid I had seen a couple of times in the ring, once when he was on the card with Solor-zano, that seemed to be their main ace at the time, and once after the

> "We learn a little about the narrator—he is broke. We like stories about people at the end of their rope."

main season was over, when he killed two bulls in a novillada they had one Sunday in the rain. He was a wow with the cape, and just moving up into the money. He had on the striped suit a Mexican thinks is pretty nifty, and a cream-colored hat. He was alone, but the managers, agents, and writers kept dropping by his table. She didn't have much of a chance, but every time three or four or five of them would shove off she would slip nearer. Pretty soon she dropped down beside him. He didn't take off his hat. That ought to have told me something, but it didn't.

Plenty of atmosphere (and accurate—I used to frequent the place!). Also we learn quite a bit about the protagonist, the narrator. There is also a feeling of tension, that something is about to happen—and it does: The narrator and Triesca have a confrontation, and the story is off and running.

ᔍ ❖ ᔐ

Mario Puzo begins his block-busting novel, *The Godfather*, with a courtroom setting and a character, but the character involved in the scene is not his protagonist; he is an undertaker and a very minor character, but Puzo slyly uses him and the scene to establish the power of the novel's focal character: Don Corleone, the Godfather.

Amerigo Bonasera sat in New York Criminal Court Number 3 and waited for justice; vengeance on the men who had so cruelly hurt his daughter, who had tried to dishonor her.

The judge, a formidably heavy-featured man, rolled up the sleeves of his black robe as if to physically chastise the two young men standing before the bench. His face was cold, with majestic contempt. But there was something false in all this that Amerigo Bonasera sensed but did not yet understand.

"You acted like the worst kind of degenerates," the judge said harshly. Yes, yes, thought Amerigo Bonasera. Animals. Animals. The two young men, glossy hair crew cut, scrubbed clean-cut faces composed into humble contrition, bowed their heads in submission.

The judge went on. "You acted like wild beasts in a jungle and you are fortunate you did not sexually molest that poor girl or I'd put you behind bars for twenty years." The judge paused, his eyes beneath impressively thick brows flickered slyly toward the sallow-faced Amerigo Bonasera, then lowered to a stack of probation reports before him. He frowned and shrugged as if convinced against his own natural desire. He spoke again.

"But because of your youth, your clean records, because of your fine families, and because the law in its majesty does not seek vengeance, I hereby sentence you to three years' confinement to the penitentiary. Sentence to be suspended."

Only forty years of professional mourning kept the overwhelming frustration and hatred from showing on Amerigo Bonasera's face. His beautiful young daughter was still in the hospital with her broken jaw wired together; and now these two *animales* went free? It had all been a farce. He watched the happy parents cluster around their darling sons. Oh, they were all happy now, they were smiling now.

The black bile, sourly bitter, rose in Bonasera's throat, overflowed through tightly clenched teeth. He used his white linen pocket handkerchief and held it against his lips. He was standing so when the two young men strode freely up the aisle, confident and cool-eyed, smiling, not giving him so much as a glance. He let them pass without saying a word, pressing the fresh linen against his mouth.

The parents of the *animales* were coming by now, two men and two women his age but more American in their dress. They glanced at him, shamefaced yet in their eyes was an odd, triumphant defiance.

The words "Italian-American" never appear, yet we sense that Bonasera feels that American justice is a legalistic farce—and readers always empathize with victims of perceived injustice. Puzo's opening scene continues:

> Out of control, Bonasera leaned forward toward the aisle and shouted hoarsely, "You will weep as I have wept—I will make you weep as your children make me weep"—the linen at his eyes now. The defense attorneys bringing up the rear swept their clients forward in a tight little band, enveloping the two young men, who had started back down the aisle as if to protect their parents. A huge bailiff moved quickly to block the row in which Bonasera stood.
>
> All his years in America, Amerigo Bonasera had trusted in law and order. And he has prospered thereby. Now though his brain smoked with hatred, though wild visions of buying a gun and killing the two young men jangled the very bones of his skull, Bonasera turned to his still uncomprehending wife and explained to her, "They have made fools of us." He paused and then made his decision, no longer fearing the cost. "For justice we must go on our knees to Don Corleone."

> **"** ...readers always empathize with victims of perceived injustice. **"**

We can be sure that once the Godfather decides to accept the assignment of retribution, those two young *animales* will wish they'd taken the three years in the penitentiary instead.

This is a highly skillful beginning to a remarkable and riveting novel, which, of course, led to a remarkable and riveting film. (Who can forget the amputated horse-head-in-the-bed scene?)

ဢ ❖ ୧ଓ

Everyone likes a quotable and surprising first line of a story or novel, viz. Ambrose Bierce's great opening of his short story, "An Imperfect Conflagration."

> Early one morning in 1872 I murdered my father—an act which made a deep impression on me at the time.

It is hard to believe that Alice Sebold, author of *The Lovely Bones*, wasn't paying homage to Bierce in her 2007 novel, *The Almost Moon*, whose first sentence is:

> When all is said and done, killing my mother came easily.

But a shocking and memorable first sentence doesn't necessarily guarantee a great story. All a good opening needs to do is pique our interest and give us a suggestion of what we are in for.

"Last night I dreamt I went to Manderlay again," is hardly a blockbuster of a first sentence, but it set the tone for one of the best suspense novels ever written, Daphne Du Maurier's 1938 *Rebecca*.

Beginning with just a setting and no interesting character in view is still practiced by some writers, and they get away with it, especially if they have a name and reputation. Salman Rushdie's 2008 novel, *The Enchantress of Florence*, begins this way:

> In the day's last light the glowing lake below the palace-city looked like a sea of molten gold....Perhaps (the traveler surmised) the fountain of eternal youth lay within the city walls—perhaps even the legendary doorway to Paradise on Earth was somewhere close at hand? But then the sun fell below

the horizon, the gold sank beneath the water's surface, and was lost. Mermaids and serpents would guard it until the return of daylight.

This beginning seems like something out of the 1920s or a parody, and I don't recommend emulating it (unless your name is Rushdie).

හ ❖ ශ

Here is a good example of character-plus-setting which tells us where we are and who we are concerned with and, though seemingly innocuous, it provides just a hint of the conflict to come. Entitled "Married Love," this story by Tessa Hadley ran in a 2007 issue of the *New Yorker*. Not only do we have the setting and characters and some conflict, we even have a little weather—a very little weather.

> Lottie announced that she was getting married.
>
> This was at the breakfast table at her parents' house one weekend. The kitchen in that house was upstairs, its windows overlooking the garden below. It was a tall, thin, old house, comfortably untidy, worn to fit the shape of the family. The summer morning was rainy, so all the lights were on, the atmosphere close and dreamy, perfumed with toast and coffee.
>
> "Whatever for?" Lottie's mother, Hattie, said, and carried on reading her book. She was an English teacher, but she read crime novels at weekends: this one was about a detective in Venice.
>
> Lottie was nineteen, but she looked more like thirteen or fourteen. She was just over five feet tall, with a tight little figure and a barrel chest; she insisted on wearing the same glasses with thick black frames that she had chosen years earlier, and her hair, the color of washed-out straw, was pulled into pigtails.
>
> Everyone happened to be at home that weekend, even Lottie's older brother, Rufus, and her sister, Em, who had moved away.
>
> "Have you got a boyfriend at last?" Em asked.
>
> Lottie was always pale, with milky translucent skin behind an arc of ghost freckles across her snub nose, but she seemed

to be even whiter than usual that morning, blue veins standing out at her temples; she clenched her hands on either side of the placemat in front of her. They were improbable hands for a violinist: pink and plump, with short blunt fingers and bitten cuticles.

"You're not taking me seriously!" she cried.

A squall of rain urged against the steamed-up windowpanes, the kettle boiled, toast sprang from the toaster for no one in particular. Vaguely, they all looked at her, thinking their own thoughts. Lottie emanated intensity; her personality was like a demon trapped inside a space too small. Even as a baby she had been preternaturally perceptive and judgmental. Her talent for the violin, when it was discovered, had seemed an explanation for her surplus strength, or a solution to it; she had begun on an instrument so tiny that it looked like a Christmas-tree decoration. Now she was living with her parents while she studied for her music degree at the university.

"Why ever would you want to get married?" Hattie said reasonably. "Dad and I have never felt the need."

"I'm not like you," Lottie said.

How very much we have learned about this family in a short time! And we are once again reminded of one of the great first lines in all literature, Tolstoy's beginning of *Anna Karenina*:

> Happy families are all alike; unhappy families are unhappy for different reasons.

We will get back to Count Leo's beginnings later, but now let us move on to an almost foolproof way to begin a novel or story: *Dialogue*

> ✔ As Elmore Leonard has said:
>
> "Readers don't skip dialogue."

4

Dialogue

Dialogue is simply a conversation between: one character and himself ("to be or not to be"), or one character with another (*Private Lives*) or several characters with each other (*Twelve Angry Men*).

It is an old, lively, and energizing way to begin a story or novel.

Hemingway liked the form and used it frequently. Here is the way he starts his famous and, at the time (1933), shocking, short story "The Sea Change." It begins with no preamble or setting:

> "All right," said the man. "What about it?"
> "No," said the girl, "I can't."
> "You mean you won't."
> "I can't," said the girl. "That's all that I mean."
> "You mean that you won't."
> "All right," said the girl. "You have it your own way."
> "I don't have it my own way. I wish to God I did."
> "You did for a long time," the girl said.

We don't know what's going on here.

Why are we hooked?

We are always hooked when we hear two people quarreling who shouldn't be; if we are in a restaurant and overhear one nearby couple quarrelling and another couple happily chatting about their children, which one do we eavesdrop on? Human nature!

We don't know who these people are in "The Sea Change" or even where we are—but we read on because *something* is going on and they are in *CONFLICT!*

In the next paragraph we learn a little more factual stuff.

> It was early, and there was no one in the café except the barman and these two who sat together at a table in the corner. It was the end of the summer and they were both tanned, so that they looked out of place in Paris. The girl wore a tweed suit, her skin was a smooth gold brown, her blond hair was cut short and grew beautifully away from her forehead. The man looked at her.
>
> "I'll kill her," he said.

> **"We are always hooked when we hear two people quarreling who shouldn't be...."**

—and then we're back to pure dialogue.

As the story goes on, all in very believable and bitter talk, we gather that the girl is leaving the man for another woman.

Many of Hemingway's best stories begin straight off with dialogue, such as his classic "The Snows of Kilimanjaro:"

> "The marvelous thing is that it's painless," he said. "That's how you know when it starts."
>
> "Is it really?"
>
> "Absolutely. I'm awfully sorry about the odor though. That must bother you."
>
> "Don't! Please don't."
>
> "Look at them," he said. "Now is it sight or is it scent that brings them like that?"

We don't know where we are or who and what we are dealing with here, but little by little we gather what is going on, and it is not a good situation.

> The cot the man lay on was in the wide shade of a mimosa tree and as he looked out past the shade onto the glare of the plain there were three of the big birds squatted obscenely, while in the sky a dozen more sailed, making quick-moving shadows as they passed.

Sometimes Hemingway starts with a single sentence of exposition before going into dialogue. Consider the following fine first sentence from the beginning of one of Hemingway's greatest short stories, "The Short Happy Life of Francis Macomber." How much the writer gets into those two dozen words!

> It was now lunch time and they were all sitting under the double green fly of the dining tent pretending that nothing had happened.
>
> "Will you have lime juice or lemon squash?" Macomber asked.
>
> "I'll have a gimlet," Robert Wilson told him.
>
> "I'll have a gimlet too. I need something," Macomber's wife said.
>
> "I suppose it's the thing to do," Macomber agreed. "Tell him to make three gimlets."

"—pretending that nothing had happened"—that, of course, makes us sit up and *have* to find out what was so terrible that they couldn't even talk about it, but quickly order drinks and make small talk. There's tension in the air, and it gets worse—much worse—and builds to a violent ending in which one of these gimlet drinkers will be murdered.

Scott Fitzgerald also liked to begin stories with dialogue, but his stories were different from the macho Hemingway type of story, so his dialogue was tamer. "Babylon Revisited," his famous story about a reformed drunk American, Charles Wales, who returns to the Paris of his playboy days in order to regain custody of his young daughter, begins quite quietly, but sets the scene for what is to come:

> "And where's Mr. Campbell?" Charlie asked.
>
> "Gone to Switzerland. Mr. Campbell's a pretty sick man, Mr. Wales."
>
> "I'm sorry to hear that. And George Hardt?" Charlie inquired.
>
> "Back in America, gone to work."
>
> "And where is the Snow Bird?"
>
> "He was in here last week. Anyway, his friend, Mr. Schaeffer, is in Paris."

Two familiar names from the long list of a year and a half ago. Charlie scribbled an address in his notebook and tore out the page.

"If you see Mr. Schaeffer, give him this," he said. "It's my brother-in-law's address. I haven't settled on a hotel yet."

He was not really disappointed to find Paris was so empty. But the stillness in the Ritz bar was strange and portentous. It was not an American bar any more—he felt polite in it, and not as if he owned it. It had gone back into France. He felt the stillness from the moment he got out of the taxi and saw the doorman, usually in a frenzy of activity at this hour, gossiping with a *chasseur* by the servants' entrance.

This is not exactly a grabber of a beginning, but it is *right* for this particular story. It sets the *tone* of what is a poignant story of a damaged man.

Robert B. Parker likes to begin his suspenseful novels with a brief expository paragraph and then jump into lively dialogue, usually a confrontational—not comfortable—one between Spenser and another character. His 2007 novel, *Now and Then*, begins:

He came into my office carrying a thin briefcase under his left arm. He was wearing a dark suit and a white shirt with a red-and-blue-striped tie. His red hair was cut very short. He had a thin, sharp face. He closed the door carefully behind him and turned and gave me the hard eye.

"You Spenser?" he said.

"And proud of it," I said.

He looked at me aggressively and didn't say anything. I smiled pleasantly.

"Are you being a wise guy?" he said.

"Only for a second," I said. "What can I do for you?"

"I don't like this," he said.

"Well," I said. "It's a start."

"I don't like funny either," he said.

"Then we should do great," I said.

"My name is Dennis Doherty," he said.

"I love alliteration," I said.

"What?"

"There I go again," I said.

"Listen, pal. You don't want my business, just say so."

"I don't want your business," I said.

He stood and walked toward my door. He opened it and stopped and turned around.

"I came on a little strong," he said.

"I noticed that," I said.

"Lemme start over," Doherty said.

I nodded.

"Try not to frighten me," I said.

He closed the door and came back and sat in one of the chairs in front of my desk. He looked at me for a time. No aggression. Just taking notice.

"You ever box?" he said.

I nodded.

"The nose?" I said.

"More around the eyes," Doherty said.

"Observant," I said.

"The nose has been broken," Doherty said. "I can see that. But it's not flattened."

"I retired before it got flat," I said.

Notice how we subtly get a look at the narrator—he has a broken nose but, more than that, we learn that in the past he was a minor boxer.

It is always a problem how—when writing in the first person—to let the reader know what the person telling the story looks like. The usual device is a store window or a mirror—"not a bad figure for a forty-year-old gal with two kids," etc.

In the above example, the writer uses the minor character to tell us what the narrator and protagonist looks like; it is a time-honored trick.

In the many pages of dialogue that follow Parker's opening, we learn Doherty's problem. He's actually a pretty nice guy who's got a problem—he adores his wife and is afraid she's having an affair, and he wants Spenser to find out. She is—and he does. Parker's charming books depend less on plot and more on characterization—*and sparkling dialogue!*

ஸ் ❖ ௸

Ideally, good dialogue subtly imparts information, reveals character, and advances the plot. Elmore Leonard is an expert at realistic dialogue, as the beginning of his novel *Freaky Deakey* reveals:

> Chris Mankowski's last day on the job, two in the afternoon, two hours to go, he got a call to dispose of a bomb.
>
> What happened, a guy by the name of Booker, a twenty-five-year-old super-dude twice-convicted felon, was in his Jacuzzi when the phone rang. He yelled for his bodyguard Juicy Mouth to take it. "Hey, Juicy?" His bodyguard, his driver and his houseman were around somewhere. "Will somebody get the phone?" The phone kept ringing. The phone must have rung fifteen times before Booker got out of the Jacuzzi, put on his green satin robe that matched the emerald pinned to his left earlobe and picked up the phone. Booker said, "Who's this?" A woman's voice said, "You sitting down?" The phone was on a table next to a green leather wingback chair. Booker loved green. He said, "Baby, is that you?" It sounded like his woman, Moselle. Her voice said, "Are you sitting down? You have to be sitting down for when I tell you something." Booker said, "Baby, you sound different. What's wrong?" He sat down in the green leather chair, frowning, working his butt around to get comfortable. The woman's voice said, "Are you sitting down?" Booker said, "I *am*. I have sat the fuck down. Now you gonna talk to me, what?" Moselle's voice said, "I'm suppose to tell you that when you get up, honey, what's left of your ass is gonna go clear through the ceiling."

Yes, there are several sticks of dynamite under Booker's chair, set to go off when he gets up, and, as it turns out, he has to go to the bathroom very badly and wants to get up—has to get up—desperately. What reader could resist reading on?

Besides being a model of how to begin this sort of a novel, there are other things to be learned from Leonard's excerpt. Consider the use of the voice, for example, the tone of the writing which is set in the first punchy sentence. And look how much we learn about Booker's life and lifestyle in a minimum of words. How simple, how effective is the foreshadowing: "Baby, you sound different."

Elizabeth Bowen, the British author of such prestigious novels as *The Death of the Heart*, has written some notes on the importance of dialogue, whether used to begin a work or not:

> Dialogue requires more art than does any other constituent of the novel. Art in the *celare artem* sense. Art in the trickery, self-justifying distortion sense. Why? Because dialogue must appear realistic without being so. Actual realism—the lifting, as it were, of passages from a stenographer's take-down of a "real life" conversation—would be disruptive. Of what? Of the illusion of the novel. In "real life" everything is diluted; in the novel everything is condensed.
>
> What are the realistic qualities to be imitated (or faked) in novel dialogue?—Spontaneity. Artless or hit-or-miss arrival at words used. Ambiguity (speaker not sure, himself, what he means). Effect of choking (as in engine): more to be said than can come through. Irrelevance. Allusiveness. Erraticness: unpredictable course. Repercussion.
>
> What must novel dialogue, behind mask of these faked realistic qualities, really be and do? It must be pointed, intentional, relevant. It must crystallize situation. It must express character. It must advance plot. During dialogue, the characters confront one another. The confrontation is in itself an occasion. Each one of these occasions, throughout the novel, is unique. Since the last confrontation, something has changed, advanced. What is being said is the effect of something that has happened; at the same time, what is being said *is in itself something happening*, which will, in turn, leave its effect.
>
> Dialogue is the ideal means of showing what is between the characters. It crystallizes relationships. It *should*, ideally, be so effective as to make analysis or explanation of the relationship between the characters unnecessary. Short of a small range of physical acts—a fight, murder, lovemaking—dialogue is the most vigorous and visible interaction of which characters in a novel are capable. Speech is what characters *do to each other*.

Here is an example of some great anonymous dialogue from the seventh century B.C. that Elizabeth Bowen would approve of:

> The Laconians were sparing in speech and emotion. A foreign conqueror sent a message: "If I get to Laconia, not one brick will stand upon another."
> The laconic reply was "If."

ℰ ❖ ℬ

As for beginning a novel with *economic* dialogue, Mark Twain takes first prize. The first sentence of *The Adventures of Tom Sawyer* is simply and effectively: "Tom!" (His Aunt Polly is calling him.)

To sum up: The writer doesn't have to come up with a whamdoozler of a first sentence—such as Robertson Davies' start of *The Cunning Man*: "Should I have taken the false teeth?"

The first sentence can be as commonplace as: "Good morning," he snarled.

As Elmore Leonard has taught us, going immediately or very soon into dialogue is a very good way to start a story, since "Readers don't skip dialogue."

Let's end this chapter with Sol Stein's guidelines for dialogue from his fine book on writing, *How to Grow a Novel*:

1. What counts in dialogue is not what is said but what is meant.

2. Whenever possible, dialogue should be adversarial. Think of dialogue as confrontations or interrogations. Remember, combat can be subtle.

3. The best dialogue contains responses that are indirect, oblique.

4. Dialogue is illogical. Non sequiturs are fine. So are incomplete sentences, and occasional faulty grammar suited to the character.

5. Dialogue, compared to actual speech, is terse. If a speech runs over three sentences, you may be speechifying. In

accusatory confrontations, however, longer speeches can increase tension if the accusations build.

6. Tension can be increased by the use of misunderstandings, impatience, and especially by giving the characters in a scene different scripts.

7. Characters reveal themselves best in dialogue when they lose their cool and start blurting things out.

8. Think of the analogies with baseball and Ping-Pong as a way of understanding how dialogue differs from ordinary exchanges. In life, adversarial or heated exchanges tend to be repetitive; in dialogue, such exchanges build. In life, adversarial exchanges vent the speakers' emotions; in dialogue, such exchanges are designed to move a story forward.

9. Avoid dialect. It makes readers see words on the page and interrupts their experience.

10. In dialogue every word counts. Be ruthless in eliminating excess. All talk is first draft. Dialogue is not talk.

5

Seemingly Factual

A DISARMING WAY TO SEDUCE THE READER INTO THINKING THE story or novel actually happened is to start with what appears to be a nonfiction statement or fact.

One of the best known stories ever written starts this way. Before the first sentence in Hemingway's "The Snows of Kilimanjaro," there appears this paragraph almost as a side-bar or a newspaper clipping:

> Kilimanjaro is a snow-covered mountain 19,710 feet high, and is said to be the highest mountain in Africa. Its western summit is called by the Masai "Ngàje Ngài," the House of God. Close to the western summit there is the dried and frozen carcass of a leopard. No one has explained what the leopard was seeking at that altitude.

Then the author presents a dying man's dialogue with his wife. (Hemingway never does tell us what that leopard was doing up there!)

Years after writing the story, Hemingway would come back to that no-nonsense, straight-forward type of beginning in his novel *The Old Man and the Sea*:

> He was an old man who fished alone in a skiff in the Gulf Stream and he had gone eighty-four days now without taking a fish.

What a way to get *who*, *what*, *why*, and *where* into one sentence! I started my book *La Fiesta Brava* with this sentence:

> On August 28, 1947, a multi-millionaire and a bull killed each other in Linares, Spain, and plunged an entire nation into deep mourning.

(I was inordinately proud when Elmore Leonard, years later, told the *New York Times* that this was his all-time favorite story beginning.)

John Grisham knows the importance of beginning fast, and he likes to have the reader believe that his fiction actually happened. Take his 2008 best-seller, *The Appeal*:

> The jury was ready.
>
> After forty-two hours of deliberations that followed seventy-one days of trial that included 530 hours of testimony from four dozen witnesses, and after a lifetime of sitting silently as the lawyers haggled and the judge lectured and the spectators watched like hawks for telltale signs, the jury was ready. Locked away in the jury room, secluded and secure, ten of them proudly signed their names to the verdict while the other two pouted in their corners, detached and miserable in their dissension. There were hugs and smiles and no small measure of self-congratulation because they had survived this little war and could now march proudly back into the arena with a decision they had rescued through sheer determination and the dogged pursuit of compromise. Their ordeal was over; their civic duty complete. They had served above and beyond. They were ready.

> " John Grisham knows the importance of beginning fast, and he likes to have the reader believe that his fiction actually happened. "

We don't yet know what this trial was about, but given these hard statistics we know it was a very important one. In a few more paragraphs we meet the protagonists, the two people we will be rooting for in this novel—and in any story we must have a goal and someone to root for. Grisham's beginning continues:

> The clerk's first call went to the firm of Payton & Payton, a local husband-and-wife team now operating out of an abandoned dime store in a lesser part of town. A paralegal picked up the phone, listened for a few seconds, hung up, then shouted, "The jury has a verdict!" His voice echoed through the cavernous maze of small, temporary workrooms and jolted his colleagues.
>
> He shouted it again as he ran to The Pit, where the rest of the firm was frantically gathered. Wes Payton was already there, and when his wife, Mary Grace, rushed in, their eyes met in a split second of unbridled fear and bewilderment. Two paralegals, two secretaries, and a bookkeeper gathered at the long, cluttered worktable, where they suddenly froze and gawked at one another, all waiting for someone else to speak.
>
> Could it really be over? After they had waited for an eternity, could it end so suddenly? So abruptly? With just a phone call?
>
> "How about a moment of silent prayer," Wes said, and they held hands in a tight circle and prayed as they had never prayed before. All manner of petitions were lifted up to God Almighty, but the common plea was for victory. Please, dear Lord, after all this time and effort and money and fear and doubt, please, oh please, grant us a divine victory. And deliver us from humiliation, ruin, bankruptcy, and a host of other evils that a bad verdict will bring.

Why are we already rooting for the Paytons?

Because they are obviously a likable couple whose lives will depend upon this forthcoming verdict. If the trial's verdict goes against their client (whose husband and young son died because of a huge, ruthless chemical company's negligence) they will be ruined. They are in trouble, and we root for likable people in trouble—especially Davids against Goliaths.

A seemingly factual statement can set the tone of the entire work, as in Norman MacLean's *A River Runs Through It* (and, indeed, a river does run all through the novel):

In our family, there was no clear line between religion and fly fishing. We lived at the junction of great trout rivers in western Montana, and our father was a Presbyterian minister and a fly fisherman who tied his own flies and taught others. He told us about Christ's disciples being fishermen, and we were left to assume, as my brother and I did, that all first-class fishermen on the Sea of Galilee were fly fishermen and that John, the favorite, was a dry-fly fisherman.

Here again we have a beginning that is not exactly exciting, but it is charming and the thought presented is so civilized we want to see what the story's all about. (I enjoyed a recent scathing critique of a film by a reviewer who wrote: "This movie is somewhat like *A River Runs Through It*, except that there is no river and nothing runs through it.")

In *David Copperfield*'s beginning, Charles Dickens wants to convince the reader that this is a *true* autobiography rather than a novel:

I Am Born

Whether I shall turn out to be the hero of my own life, or whether that station will be held by anybody else, these pages must show. To begin my life with the beginning of my life, I record that I was born (as I have been informed and believe) on a Friday, at twelve o'clock at night. It was remarked that the clock began to strike, and I began to cry, simultaneously.

In consideration of the day and hour of my birth, it was declared by the nurse, and by some sage women in the neighbourhood who had taken a lively interest in me several months before there was any possibility of our becoming personally acquainted, first, that I was destined to be unlucky in life; and secondly, that I was privileged to see ghosts and spirits; both these gifts inevitably attaching, as they believed, to all unlucky infants of either gender, born towards the small hours on a Friday night.

I need say nothing here, on the first head, because nothing can show better than my history whether that prediction was verified or falsified by the result. On the second branch of the question, I will only remark, that unless I ran through that part of my inheritance while I was still a baby, I have not come into it yet. But I do not at all complain of having been kept out of this property; and if anybody else should be in the present enjoyment of it, he is heartily welcome to keep it.

I was born with a caul, which was advertised for sale, in the newspapers, at the low price of fifteen guineas. Whether sea-going people were short of money about that time, or were short of faith and preferred cork jackets, I don't know; all I know is, that there was but one solitary bidding, and that was from an attorney connected with the bill-broking business, who offered two pounds in cash, and the balance in sherry, but declined to be guaranteed from drowning on any higher bargain.

A caul is a membrane around a fetus, and apparently, in those days, if the child was born with it wrapped around its head it was considered to be a talisman guaranteed to protect sailors and anyone else from drowning.

This beginning of Frederick Forsyth's best-selling thriller, *The Day of the Jackal*, could have come from a factual newspaper report, though the novel was pure fiction:

It is cold at 6:40 in the morning of a March day in Paris, and seems even colder when a man is about to be executed by firing squad. At that hour on March 1, 1963, in the main court-yard of the Ford d'Ivry a French Air Force colonel stood before a stake driven into the chilly gravel as his hands were bound behind the post, and stared with slowly diminishing disbelief at the squad of soldiers facing him twenty metres away.

We don't know who the man is. We don't know what he has done to deserve execution. We don't know whether the sentence will be carried out.

But! … we have to find out! We will read on!

And, speaking of Paris, John Collier starts his wild 1960 story "Softly Walks the Beetle" as though it were a travel article in a Sunday newspaper or a monthly magazine:

Florian's is the resort of film and fashion, and the most successful café on the Champs-Élysées. The tables have been reduced to the size of dinner plates. They are crowded so close together that whoever leans back in his chair may receive bitter reproaches in his right ear for infidelity, and in his left for lack of understanding. If he leans forward to escape these he may find himself involved in a motion picture deal which is not likely to come off. The solitary is well advised to cower over his *apéritif,* and to fix his eyes on the sidewalk and study the passing crowd.

This could be the start of an article from the magazine *Travel and Leisure*, but Collier is too great a storyteller to stay on a static description of a restaurant, even one in Paris, for very long.

Now that he has us believing in a real place in a real city, he shifts gears, and we know we are reading fiction when we meet the young protagonist:

I had no sooner made this depressing discovery, than the corner of a newspaper hovered over my coffee, and the radar in my ribs warned me of an elbow at a distance of not more than three inches. I glanced to my right. At the table between my own and the planting box was seated a young man who had all the look of one of the new bohemians, the more or less juvenile delinquents of the international motion picture set. As all arts tend to the condition of music, so the pants of these young men, whatever may be their cut or material, tend to the condition of Levis. Their haircuts tend to the crewcut. Their shoes are so easygoing as to constitute, when worn in the presence of strangers, an impudent familiarity. Too numerous wherever they are, these young men are most numerous at film festivals, where they crowd the foyers of the best hotels, translating them into lobbies. Their wagons are sometimes hitched to a star; more often to a director. Their services are available; there is little they cannot, and nothing they will not, do.

Reason now whispered reassuringly that he might, after all, be only, as we used to say of assistant producers in Hollywood, a mouse with ambitions to become a rat.

The story progresses now with the entrance of the antagonist, who we believe at first to be a harmless, bumbling old fogey.

While I was still wondering to which order this particular specimen belonged, my attention was diverted by the apparition of an elderly gentleman who, even while he approached us in the main stream of passers-by, seemed, by reason of his improbable size and splendor, to move more slowly than the rest of them. It is thus that a great liner seems almost motionless in comparison with the scurrying tugs amidst whom, and at precisely the same speed, she moves majestically to her mooring.

This gentleman halted at our corner of the *terrasse*, and his rather puffy lips trembled a little as he looked over the wide expanse of tables. The crowd was crushed as close as a swarm of bees, buzzing with love and crawling with money, and there was not a single gap to be seen.

The old boy addressed the oaf who was sitting by the planting box. "I wonder if you'd very much mind if I sat at your table. I promise you I won't be in the very least a nuisance." These words were uttered in a tone of the humblest supplication; one of the very few things that were better for being obviously a fake. (One can get the genuine article from any panhandler.) The bland humility was spiced by a twinkling glance of good fellowship, sparkling from under an eyebrow whose naughty lift suggested that only an amusing mischance could have brought these two together in a place which, though probably respectable enough; was not exactly the Jockey Club.

All these delightful nuances were completely wasted on my neighbor. With one shoe half off and half on, he lifted his nose half out of his gossip column, which he was studying as earnestly as a punter studies a form sheet, and he signified with half a grunt and half a nod that he had no objection to the stranger taking the vacant chair.

The old boy lowered his vast posterior onto the inadequate little seat with a sigh of relief. He made no attempt to summon a waiter, but folded his hands over the handle of his mighty cane, and demurely dropped his eyes upon them. They were large, expensive, leathery looking hands, and their leatheriness was of such a quality as to make it clear that, regardless of any little prejudice you and I may entertain, the finest article in that line is made from human skin. These hands, moreover, were adorned with three or four enormous rings, and in each of these rings was a diamond of such implausible size that no maker of imitation jewelry could possibly have had the effrontery to concoct it.

The Faustian story proceeds, always in the café, and little by little, we realize the old boy isn't just a nice old man, but is after the ambitious young man's soul, and how he cleverly succeeds is the thrust of a brilliant and weird tale. The reader is given a few subtle clues along the way, but not till the end are we aware that the codger is Lucifer in disguise.

And all this started with a beginning that we thought was a travelogue!

6

Interrogatory

Perhaps the first great work to begin by asking a question was written by Shakespeare who begins his classic drama *Hamlet* with a very modern and grabbing device—a sentinel in the castle at Elsinore calls out:

"Who's there?"

It is the ghost of Hamlet's father who was murdered by Hamlet's uncle.

Almost equally brief is the Bard's first line from *Macbeth*:

"When shall we three meet again?"

Beginning with a question has been popular in every genre—even in juvenile literature. *Alice's Adventure in Wonderland* starts with this long sentence, which ends with an interrogatory:

> Alice was beginning to get very tired of sitting by her sister on the bank and of having nothing to do: once or twice she had peeped into the book her sister was reading, but it had no pictures or conversations in it, "and what is the use of a book," thought Alice, "without pictures or conversations?"

And even E.B. White's lovely *Charlotte's Web* begins with a question—and a hint of violence:

"Where's Papa going with that ax?" said Fern to her mother as they were setting the table for breakfast.

"Out to the hoghouse," replied Mrs. Arable. "Some pigs were born last night."

"I don't see why he needs an ax," continued Fern, who was only eight.

"Well," said her mother, "one of the pigs is a runt. It's very small and weak, and it will never amount to anything. So your father has decided to do away with it."

"Do *away* with it," shrieked Fern. "You mean *kill* it? Just because it's smaller than the others?"

Mrs. Arable put a pitcher of cream on the table.

"Don't yell, Fern!" she said. "Your father is right. The pig would probably die anyway."

Fern pushed a chair out of the way and ran outdoors. The grass was wet and the earth smelled of springtime. Fern's sneakers were sopping by the time she caught up with her father.

"Please don't kill it!" she sobbed. "It's unfair."

Mr. Arable stopped walking.

"Fern," he said gently, "you will have to learn to control yourself."

"Control myself?" yelled Fern. "This is a matter of life and death, and you talk about *controlling* myself." Tears ran down her cheeks and she took hold of the ax and tried to pull it out of her father's hand.

"Fern," said Mr. Arable, "I know more about raising a litter of pigs than you do. A weakling makes trouble. Now run along!"

> " ...even if some people don't care much about animals in real life, they rarely fail to react to their plights in fiction. "

This dramatic scene tugs at the heart; even if some people don't care much about animals in real life, they rarely fail to react to their plights in fiction.

It would be hard to top Jack London's brevity in the beginning to his strange story, "Told in the Drooling Ward."

"Me?"

The story continues:

> I'm not a drooler. I'm the assistant. I don't know what Miss Jones or Miss Kelsey could do without me.

Anthony Trollope begins his classic novel *Barchester Towers* with a question that constitutes the spine of the rest of his story:

> In the latter days of July in the year 1885, a most important question was for ten days hourly asked in the cathedral city of Barchester, and answered every hour in various ways—"Who was to be the new Bishop?"

Saul Bellow starts his 1959 novel, *Henderson the Rain King*, thusly:

> What made me take this trip to Africa? There is no explanation. Things got worse and worse and worse and pretty soon they were too complicated.

Talk about foreshadowing conflict!

Larry McMurtry starts his novel, *Some Can Whistle*, about a writer's long-lost daughter, with a strange question:

> "Mister Deck, are you my stinkin' Daddy?" a youthful, female, furious voice said into the phone.
>
> I could not have been more startled if I had looked up into the blue Texas sky and seen a nuclear bomb on its way down. I was on my south patio, having breakfast with Godwin, watching the fine peachy light of an early summer morning spread over the prairies; I had assumed the call was from my agent, who was in Paris and would soon be swimming up the time zones, hoping to spawn a few deals.
>
> "I don't think I stink," I said politely.

Erich Segal's tear-jerking bestseller of yesteryear, *Love Story*, asked the question:

> What can you say about a twenty-five-year-old girl who died?

(One cynical critic wrote of this beginning: "Well, you *could* say she'll never see twenty-six!")

It is hard to conceive of a more chilling beginning for a tale of horror than that of Edgar Allan Poe's "The Tell-Tale Heart," written in 1843.

> True!—nervous—very, very dreadfully nervous I had been and am! But why will you say that I am mad? The disease had sharpened my senses—not destroyed—not dulled them. Above all was the sense of hearing acute. I heard all things in the heaven and in the earth. I heard many things in hell. How, then am I mad?

(Poe is generally credited with inventing the detective story when he wrote "Murders in the Rue Morgue.")

Evelyn Waugh starts his brilliant novel, *A Handful of Dust*, with the question:

> "Was anyone hurt?"

Somerset Maugham starts his novel *Painted Veil* with a quick remark, followed by a question:

> She gave a startled cry.
> "What's the matter?" he asked.
> Notwithstanding the darkness of the shuttered room he saw her face on a sudden distraught with terror.
> "Some one just tried the door."
> "Well, perhaps it was the amah, or one of the boys."
> "They never come at this time. They know I always sleep after tiffin."
> "Who else could it be?"
> "Walter," she whispered, her lips trembling.

She pointed to his shoes. He tried to put them on, but his nervousness, for her alarm was affecting him, made him clumsy, and besides, they were on the tight side. With a faint gasp of impatience she gave him a shoe horn. She slipped into a kimono and in her bare feet went over to her dressing-table. Her hair was shingled and with a comb she had repaired its disorder before he had laced his second shoe. She handed him his coat.

"How shall I get out?"

"You'd better wait a bit. I'll look out and see that it's all right."

"It can't possibly be Walter. He doesn't leave the laboratory till five."

"Who is it then?"

They spoke in whispers now. She was quaking. It occurred to him that in an emergency she would lose her head and on a sudden he felt angry with her. If it wasn't safe why the devil had she said it was? She caught her breath and put her hand on his arm. He followed the direction of her glance. They stood facing the windows that led out on the verandah. They were shuttered and the shutters were bolted. They saw the white china knob of the handle slowly turn. They had heard no one walk along the verandah. It was terrifying to see that silent motion. A minute passed and there was no sound. Then, with the ghastliness of the supernatural, in the same stealthy, noiseless, and horrifying manner, they saw the white china knob of the handle at the other window turn also. It was so frightening that Kitty, her nerves failing her, opened her mouth to scream but, seeing what she was going to do, he swiftly put his hand over it and her cry was smothered in his fingers.

Would a reader put either of the two previously cited books down after those beginnings?

ജ ❖ ൠ

A caution: Remember that no matter how arresting a beginning you come up with, it can't make a great story by itself—it can only get your reader *into* your tale, which better be a good one.

When I was very young, I wrote what I thought was a splendid beginning:

> When did I start to suspect?
> I guess I first began to feel uneasy in my marriage when I came upon Margie in the basement making a small but workable guillotine.

Wow, I thought.

Unfortunately, I had no idea what the rest of the story was about, so the masterpiece was abandoned forever—great literature's loss.

Margaret Millar, the fine writer of mysteries in her later life, wrote a poetic first line at eleven years of age that haunted her for the rest of her life:

> "Oh, but what is death except an end to idle breathing?"
> "I've been worrying all these years," she lamented to me once. "Where does it go from there?"

Where indeed?

છ ❖ ૪

To Have and Have Not is not considered one of Hemingway's better novels, but it has an arresting beginning. It is also interesting and unusual because the novel consists of three parts, each of which has a different viewpoint: first person, third person, and omniscient. It begins with a rhetorical question:

> You know how it is there early in the morning in Havana with the bums still asleep against the walls of the buildings; before even the ice wagons come by with ice for the bars? Well, we came across the square from the dock to the Pearl of San Francisco Café to get coffee and there was only one beggar awake in the square and he was getting a drink out of the fountain. But when we got inside the café and sat down, there were the three of them waiting for us.
> We sat down and one of them came over.

"Well," he said.

"I can't do it," I told him. "I'd like to do it as a favor. But I told you last night I couldn't."

"You can name your own price."

"It isn't that. I can't do it. That's all."

The two others had come over and they stood there looking sad. They were nice-looking fellows all right and I would have liked to have done them the favor.

"A thousand apiece," said the one who spoke good English.

"Don't make me feel bad," I told him. "I tell you true I can't do it."

Why is this a good beginning for a story?

We have no idea what "it" is that the three men want our protagonist to do—*but!*—he doesn't want to do it! Or is afraid to do it!

Whenever you have a situation where someone wants something badly and someone else opposes it vigorously, you have—*Conflict!*

And the reader is immediately interested.

7

In Medias Res

LET'S GET TO THE NITTY-GRITTY.

Classics are fine, *but*: How do most best-selling writers today start their stories or novels?

They start *in medias res*!

Which simply is a fancy Latin way of saying they plunge into the middle of things, into an intense scene of—Something Happening!

Max Shulman parodies this type of beginning in his comic novel *Rally Round the Flag, Boys!*:

> Bang.
> Bang.
> Bang.
> Three shots ripped through my groin, and I was off on the
> biggest adventure of my life.

Shulman is being funny here, but the truth is his spoof is not so very different from, say, the beginning of a Robert Ludlum, Ed McBain, Lee Child, or Harlan Coben novel.

Years ago, the great Eudora Welty reminisced at our Santa Barbara Writers Conference: "I remember I opened a story with this sentence: 'Monsieur Boule inserted a delicate dagger in Mademoiselle's left side and departed with a poised immediacy.' I like to think I didn't take myself seriously then—but I did."

We do not need to have pistols or daggers to have an *in medias res* beginning—we simply need to be in the middle of *a situation*, even if it's only a domestic quarrel, a la Edward Albee's *Who's Afraid of Virginia Woolf?*

Almost all Hemingway stories and novels start *in medias res*, not necessarily in the first sentence, but certainly on the first page. And though famous for his action and adventure stories, some Hemingway stories are quiet tales. But they all have something that makes you want to read on. Let's look at some.

"The Last Good Country" begins with this exchange:

> "Nickie," his sister said to him. "Listen to me, Nickie."
> "I don't want to hear it."

Notice how the writer injects a small conflict right off the bat; if Nickie had answered "Tell me all about it, Sis!" we wouldn't get involved—now we want to find out what he doesn't want to hear. The story goes on:

> He was watching the bottom of the spring where the sand rose in small spurts with the bubbling water. There was a tin cup on a forked stick that was stuck in the gravel by the spring and Nick Adams looked at it and at the water rising and then flowing clear in its gravel bed beside the road.
>
> He could see both ways on the road and he looked up the hill and then down to the dock and the lake, the wooded point across the bay and the open lake beyond where there were white caps running. His back was against a big cedar tree and behind him there was a thick cedar swamp. His sister was sitting on the moss beside him and she had her arm around his shoulders.
>
> "They're waiting for you to come home to supper," his sister said. "There's two of them. They came in a buggy and they asked where you were."
>
> "Did anybody tell them?"
>
> "Nobody knew where you were but me. Did you get many, Nickie?"
>
> "I got twenty-six."

Do we know what's going on? Not the foggiest, but *something* is happening, and that something is clearly important to the protagonists.

> ✔ If the problem or the situation isn't important to the characters, it won't be important to the reader either!

Of course Hemingway usually starts with action, often violent action, as in the first sentence of his story, "After the Storm:"

> It wasn't about anything, something about making punch, and then we started fighting and I slipped and he had me down kneeling on my chest and choking me with both hands like he was trying to kill me and all the time I was trying to get the knife out of my pocket to cut him loose. Everybody was too drunk to pull him off me. He was choking me and hammering my head on the floor and I got the knife out and opened it up; and I cut the muscle right across his arm and he let go of me. He couldn't have held on if he wanted to. Then he rolled and hung onto that arm and started to cry and I said:
>
> "What the hell you want to choke me for?"
>
> I'd have killed him.

> 66 Do we know what's going on? Not the foggiest, but *something* is, and it is clearly important to the protagonists. 99

Who are these people? Where are they? Why do we care?
We don't know, but we are *there* with them and want to know more.

℘ ❖ ℭ

In his story "Now I Lay Me," Hemingway starts uncharacteristically with rumination, which is often a boring and deadly way to begin a story, but in Hemingway's hands it works:

That night we lay on the floor in the room and I listened to the silk-worms eating. The silk-worms fed in racks of mulberry leaves and all night you could hear them eating and a dropping sound in the leaves. I myself did not want to sleep because I had been living for a long time with the knowledge that if I ever shut my eyes in the dark and let myself go, my soul would go out of my body. I had been that way for a long time, ever since I had been blown up at night and felt it go out of me and go off and then come back.

Hemingway's beginning of "In Another Country" is often cited as a model of how to make a static description of a place come alive through specific details:

In the fall the war was always there, but we did not go to it any more. It was cold in the fall in Milan and the dark came very early. Then the electric lights came on, and it was pleasant along the streets looking in the windows. There was much game hanging outside the shops, and the snow powdered in the fur of the foxes and wind blew their tails. The deer hung stiff and heavy and empty, and small birds blew in the wind and the wind turned their feathers. It was a cold fall and the wind came down from the mountains.

We were all at the hospital every afternoon, and there were different ways of walking across the town through the dusk to the hospital. Two of the ways were alongside canals, but they were long. Always, though, you crossed a bridge across a canal to enter the hospital. There was a choice of three bridges. On one of them a woman sold roasted chestnuts. It was warm, standing in front of her charcoal fire, and the chestnuts were warm afterward in your pocket.

But we did not go to it any more!

There is so much to be learned from Hemingway's beginnings, almost all of which begin *in medias res*. Let's look at some more.

"A Way You'll Never Be" starts:

The attack had gone across the field, been held up by machine-gun fire from the sunken road and from the group of farm houses, encountered no resistance in the town, and reached the bank of the river. Coming along the road on a bicycle, getting off to push the machine when the surface of the road became too broken, Nicholas Adams saw what had happened by the position of the dead.

They lay alone or in clumps in the high grass of the field and along the road, their pockets out, and over them were flies and around each body or group of bodies were the scattered papers.

Hemingway is always good on small details, like "their pockets out," "scattered papers," implying, not telling, that they'd been picked over by the enemy.

It's not easy to explain the magic of Hemingway's way with *in medias res* beginnings. For example, why are we interested in this story where, theoretically, nothing is happening?

The famous story "A Clean Well-Lighted Place" starts:

It was late and every one had left the café except an old man who sat in the shadow the leaves of the tree made against the electric light. In the day time the street was dusty, but at night the dew settled the dust and the old man liked to sit late because he was deaf and now at night it was quiet and he felt the difference. The two waiters inside the café knew that the old man was a little drunk, and while he was a good client they knew that if he became too drunk he would leave without paying, so they kept watch on him.

"Last week he tried to commit suicide," one waiter said.

"Why?"

"He was in despair."

"What about?"

"Nothing."

"How do you know it was nothing?"

"He has plenty of money."

Nothing's happening, but we have the feeling something's going to—and as in all Hemingway stories—it does.

Animals play a big part in Hemingway's writings. Witness the beginning of "An African Story:"

> He was waiting for the moon to rise and he felt Kibo's hair rise under his hand as he stroked him to be quiet and they both watched and listened as the moon came up and gave them shadows. His arm was around the dog's neck now and he could feel him shivering. All of the night sounds had stopped. They did not hear the elephant and David did not see him until the dog turned his head and seemed to settle into David. Then the elephant's shadow covered them and he moved past making no noise at all and they smelled him in the light wind that came down from the mountain. He smelled strong but old and sour and when he was past David saw that the left tusk was so long it seemed to reach the ground.

The opening of Hemingway's great novel *For Whom the Bell Tolls* is vintage and classic *in medias res* style:

> He lay flat on the brown, pine-needled floor of the forest, his chin on his folded arms, and high overhead the wind blew in the tops of the pine trees. The mountainside sloped gently where he lay; but below it was steep and he could see the dark of the oiled road winding through the pass. There was a stream alongside the road and far down the pass he saw a mill beside the stream and the falling water of the dam, white in the summer sunlight.

We don't know who this guy is or what he's doing lying in a forest somewhere. But he is alert and seems to be watching and waiting for something about to happen. We will wait with him because he is in the middle of *something happening*.

So far this has turned out to be a Hemingway-full chapter—but who better to learn *in medias res* techniques from!?

ↄ ❧ Ↄ

Well, for one, there's Cormac McCarthy, who regularly starts his novels *in medias res*, viz. the first page of *All the Pretty Horses*:

> The candleflame and the image of the candleflame caught in the pierglass twisted and righted when he entered the hall and again when he shut the door. He took off his hat and came slowly forward. The floorboards creaked under his boots. In his black suit he stood in the dark glass where the lilies leaned so palely from their waisted cutglass vase. Along the cold hallway behind him hung the portraits of forebears only dimly known to him all framed in glass and dimly lit above the narrow wainscoting. He looked down at the guttered candlestub. He pressed his thumbprint in the warm wax pooled on the oak veneer. Lastly he looked at the face so caved and drawn among the folds of funeral cloth, the yellowed moustache, the eyelids paper thin. That was not sleeping. That was not sleeping.
>
> It was dark outside and cold and no wind. In the distance a calf bawled. He stood with his hat in his hand. You never combed your hair that way in your life, he said.

Who is "he," and who is the dead man he has come to view? The author will take his time filling us in—as they say, he *knows* he had us at hello.

The same with Robert Ludlum's *The Bourne Identity*:

> The trawler plunged into the angry swells of the dark, furious sea like an awkward animal trying desperately to break out of an impenetrable swamp.

The boat is in trouble—but who is on the boat?

And what is going on here in the opening of John Grisham's suspenseful novel *The Pelican Brief*?

> He seemed incapable of creating such chaos, but much of what he saw below could be blamed on him. And that was fine. He was ninety-one, paralyzed, strapped in a wheelchair and hooked to oxygen. His second stroke seven years ago had almost finished him off, but Abraham Rosenberg was still

alive and even with tubes in his nose his legal stick was bigger than the other eight. He was the only legend remaining on the Court, and the fact that he was still breathing irritated most of the mob below.

We won't know until we read further.

And who would guess that this beginning would lead us to Stephen King's horror story, *The Shining*:

Jack Torrance thought: *Officious little prick.*

But, as we've pointed out, starting in the middle of things does not necessarily mean starting with a protagonist in a dangerous or even unpleasant conflict. An *interesting small human situation* in the right hands can be made more compelling to a reader—or audience—than, say, starting in the middle of a robbery or a tornado or a battle scene.

8

Generalization

STARTING A STORY WITH A GENERALIZATION, A TRUISM, AN aphorism, a commonplace observation, or a statistic is a tried-and-true way to begin a story.

But! There are certain caveats!

We have already cited the best known of this type of beginning, Leo Tolstoy's first sentence of his great novel *Anna Karenina*:

> Happy families are all alike; every unhappy family is un-happy in its own way.

A very interesting observation, but does Tolstoy dwell on this thought and expand it?

No—he is first and foremost a storyteller and this is not an essay or a tract—this is a novel! It is a work of fiction, a story. So the old pro immediately goes to a scene involving *people* in conflict. It involves a dramatic exchange between Anna's brother and his wife.

> Everything was in confusion in the Oblonsky household. The wife had discovered that the husband was carrying on an affair with their former governess....

This would be a good beginning even in today's fiction.

In a similar vein, Somerset Maugham starts his 1931 novel, *Cakes and Ale*, with an acute observation:

I have noticed that when someone asks for you on the telephone and, finding you out, leaves a message begging you to call him up the moment you come in, as it's important, the matter is more often important to him than to you. When it comes to making you a present or doing you a favour most people are able to hold their impatience within reasonable bounds.

Then, like Tolstoy, Maugham immediately goes to a story—*the* story—which is about a famous writer and his wife, Rosie, viz.:

So when I got back to my lodgings with just enough time to have a drink, a cigarette, and to read my paper before dressing for dinner, and was told by Miss Fellows, my landlady, that Mr. Alroy Kear wishes me to ring him up at once, I felt that I could safely ignore his request.

꒰ ❖ ꒱

Maugham began several of his stories with generalities, usually keen observations of human behavior. Here is the beginning of his story "The Lotus Eater:"

Most people, the vast majority in fact, lead the lives that circumstances have thrust upon them, and though some repine, looking upon themselves as round pegs in square holes, and think that if things had been different they might have made a much better showing, the greater part accept their lot, if not with serenity, at all events with resignation. They are like tramcars traveling forever on the selfsame rails. They go backward and forward, backward and forward, inevitably, till they can go no longer and then are sold as scrap iron. It is not often that you find a man who has boldly taken the course of his life into his own hands. When you do, it is worth while having a good look at him.

And then, to quickly engage the reader's attention further, the old pro Maugham introduces a character:

That was why I was curious to meet Thomas Wilson. It was an interesting and a bold thing he had done. Of course the end was not yet, and until the experiment was concluded it was impossible to call it successful. But from what I had heard it seemed he must be an odd sort of fellow, and I thought I should like to know him. I had been told he was reserved, but I had a notion that with patience and tact I could persuade him to confide in me. I wanted to hear the facts from his own lips. People exaggerate, they love to romanticize, and I was quite prepared to discover that his story was not nearly so singular as I had been led to believe.

And this impression was confirmed when at last I made his acquaintance. It was on the Piazza in Capri....

—and we are, finally, off and running with *a story*, which is why we picked up the book in the first place.

This type of beginning has been with us for a long time—almost everyone is familiar with Jane Austen's ancient and wonderful first sentence of her novel *Pride and Prejudice*.

It is a truth universally acknowledged that a simple man in possession of a good fortune must be in want of a wife.

Then Austin immediately goes into a scene.

Paul Theroux's opening sentence of his 2001 novel, *Hotel Honolulu*, is:

Nothing to me is so erotic as a hotel room, and therefore so penetrated with life and death.

And then Theroux immediately starts his story:

Buddy Hamstra offered me a hotel job in Honolulu and laughed at my accepting it so quickly. I had been trying to begin a new life, as people do when they flee to distant places. Hawaii was paradise with heavy traffic. I met Sweetie in the hotel, where she was also working. One day when we were alone on the fourth floor I asked, "Do you want to make love?" and she said, "Part of me does." Why smile? At last we did it, then often, and always in the same vacant guest room, 409. Sweetie got pregnant, our daughter was born. So, within a year of arriving, I had my new life, and as the writer said after the crack-up, I found new things to care about. I was resident manager of the Hotel Honolulu, eighty rooms nibbled by rats.

ဢ ❖ ᙡ

Not too long ago Michael Chabon began a story this way in the *New Yorker* magazine:

> If you can still see how you could once have loved a person, you are still in love; an extinct love is always wholly incredible. One day not too long ago, in Laguna Beach....

Being a good storyteller, Chabon didn't elaborate; he went *right* to *a story*—using a "once upon a time" mode—and we want to know what happened that specific day in Laguna Beach that was worth writing a story about. From the tone of that beginning we have a pretty good idea that it is not going to be an adventure tale or one of violence, but of relationships.

On the other hand, Tami Hoag's beginning of the 1999 thriller, *Ashes to Ashes*, sets us up for mayhem to come; we are forewarned:

> Some killers are born. Some killers are made. And sometimes the origin of desire for homicide is lost in the tangle of roots that make an ugly childhood and a dangerous youth, so that no one may ever know if the urge was inbred or induced.

And then the author immediately goes into—*A Scene!*

> He lifts the body from the back of the Blazer like a roll of old carpet to be discarded. The soles of his boots scuff against the blacktop of the parking area, then fall nearly silent on the dead grass and hard ground. The night is balmy for November in Minneapolis. A swirling wind tosses fallen leaves. The bare branches of the trees rattle together like bags of bones.

He knows he falls into the last category of killers.

Flashing back to our earlier setting and weather talk in chapter two, notice how the author has us well hooked *before* we are told, *mercifully and briefly,* what the date, the weather, and the setting is/are.

If one decides to start with a well-worn truism, one can vary it by putting it in the mouth of a character in the story:

"Crime never pays," my grandfather used to say all the time, but then he died before my brother Alex found his true calling in life behind an automatic rifle.

Sara Gruen's first sentence of her best-selling 2007 novel, *Water for Elephants*, is disarmingly simple:

I am ninety. Or ninety-three. One or the other.

This strikes home with readers of a certain age; I can remember my own mother repeatedly asking me whether she was eighty-two or ninety-two. As the great old black baseball player-philosopher, Satchel Paige, used to say: "How old would you *be* if you didn't know how old you *wuz?*"

> ❝If one decides to start with a well-worn truism, one can vary it by putting it in the mouth of a character in the story....❞

After that intriguing beginning, Sara Gruen's narrator goes into a generalized monologue about conceptions of aging which could be deadly and—z-z-z-z—but the observations are so guileless and universal that we become interested in this old person who still has most of her marbles:

When you're five, you know your age down to the month. Even in your twenties you know how old you are. I'm twenty-three, you say, or maybe twenty-seven. But then in your thirties something strange starts to happen. It's a mere hiccup at first, an instant of hesitation. How old are you? Oh, I'm—you start confidently, but then you stop. You were going to say thirty-three, but you're not. You're thirty-five. And then you're bothered, because you wonder if this is the beginning of the end. It is, of course, but it's decades before you admit it.

You start to forget words; they're on the tip of your tongue, but instead of eventually dislodging, they stay there. You go upstairs to fetch something, and by the time you get there you can't remember what it was you were after. You call your child by the names of all your other children and finally the dog before you get to his. Sometimes you forget what day it is. And finally you forget the year....

It is a *good* beginning and, hooray, there are no sexy blondes in trouble, gun shots, or even the threat of an international plot threatening the end of the world as we know it!

So why are we interested?

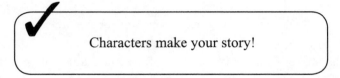

Characters make your story!

And we have, by voice alone, a character who gets our interest. What's her story?

Daddy, tell me a story, please!

And to end this chapter on that note, let us remind readers of a *very* important neglected aspect of writing which F. Scott Fitzgerald outlines in the beginning of a fictional story in the very category which we've just been talking about. It is from his long story, "The Rich Boy:"

Begin with an individual, and before you know it you find that you have created a type; begin with a type, and you find that you have created—nothing. That is because we are all queer fish, queerer behind our faces and voices than we want any one to know or than we know ourselves. When I hear a man proclaiming himself an "average, honest, open fellow," I feel pretty sure that he has some definite and perhaps terrible abnormality which he has agreed to conceal—and his protestation of being average and honest and open is his way of reminding himself of his misprision.

Then the story continues with the introduction of the eponymous rich boy, Anson, his life and problems....

Every writer should keep those first two sentences in mind—always!

My personal all-time favorite in this generalization style of beginning is L. P. Hartley's *The Go-Between*. It is brief but unforgettable:

> The past is a foreign country; they do things differently there.

Then the author starts his tale:

> When I came upon the diary it was lying at the bottom of a rather battered red cardboard collar-box, in which as a small boy I kept my Eton collars. Someone, probably my mother, had filled it with treasures dating from those days. There were two dry, empty sea-urchins; two rusty magnets, a large one and a small one, which had almost lost their magnetism; some negatives rolled up in a tight coil; some stumps of sealing-wax; a small combination lock with three rows of letters; a twist of very fine whipcord, and one or two ambiguous objects, pieces of things, of which the use was not at once apparent; I could not even tell what they had belonged to. The relics were not exactly dirty nor were they quite clean, they had the patina of age; and as I handled them, for the first time for over fifty years, a recollection of what each had meant to me came back, faint as the magnet's power to draw, but as perceptible. Something came and went between us; the intimate pleasure of recognition, the almost mystical thrill of early ownership—feelings of which, at sixty-odd, I felt ashamed.
>
> It was a roll-call in reverse; the children of the past announced their names, and I said 'Here'. Only the diary refused to disclose its identity.
>
> My first impression was that it was a present someone had brought me from abroad. The shape, the lettering, the purple limp leather curling upwards at the corners, gave it a foreign look; and it had, I could see, gold edges. Of all the exhibits it

was the only one that might have been expensive. I must have treasured it, why then could I not give it a context?

I did not want to touch it and told myself that this was because it challenged my memory; I was proud of my memory and disliked having it prompted. So I sat staring at the diary, as at a blank space in a crossword puzzle.

When a character comes across a diary—which happens quite often in fiction—what wonderful (or terrible) secrets will the reader learn?

This small but beguiling novel was made into a small but beguiling English film in 1970, starring Julie Christie, Alan Bates, and Michael Redgrave. The script was by Harold Pinter, who followed the book faithfully, *mirabile dictu*; so often filmmakers acquire a "property" because of its charm, then hire a team whose task is to identify the charming elements and eliminate them from the final product. Without giving too much away, the story is about an illicit affair peripherally observed by the narrator as a young boy, but it ultimately is about love and the loss of innocence, two of the most potent and enduring themes in fiction.

9

Author to Reader

In this way of beginning, the author talks chattily to the reader as though they were in a room together.

"Lissen, I've got a great story to tell you—"

And it's absolutely true!

Addressing the reader directly is a sly way of luring the reader into one's story, viz. Holden Caulfield in J.D. Salinger's perennial best-seller of 1951, *The Catcher in the Rye*:

> If you really want to hear about it, the first thing you'll probably want to know is where I was born, and what my lousy childhood was like, and how my parents were occupied and all before they had me, and all that David Copperfield kind of crap, but I don't feel like going into it, if you want to know the truth.

At the time of its publication, this was considered an unusual way of starting a story; people tended to forget its many antecedents, such as Poe's "The Tell-Tale Heart":

> True!—nervous—very, very dreadfully nervous I had been and am! But why *will* you say that I am mad?

or Herman Melville's cozy invitation at the start of *Moby Dick*: "Call me Ishmael."

(I think I prefer Peter De Vries' beginning to his parody, *Vale of Laughter*: "Call me, Ishmael. Feel absolutely free to do so.")

Mark Twain's artful opening to *The Adventures of Huckleberry Finn* sets the tone for one of the most important books in American literature:

> You don't know about me without you have read a book by the name of *The Adventures of Tom Sawyer*, but that ain't no matter. That book was made by Mr. Mark Twain and he told the truth, mainly. There was things which he stretched, but mainly he told the truth. That is nothing. I never seen anybody but lied one time or another, without it was Aunt Polly or the widow, or maybe Mary. Aunt Polly—Tom's Aunt Polly, she is—and Mary and the Widow Douglas is all told about in that book, which is mostly a true book, with some stretchers as I said before.

This is not a children's book, like its twin, *Tom Sawyer*; this is a book for every aspiring writer; so much can be learned from Twain's characterizations, plotting, and overall humanity. Nowadays, the tendency is for the author to stay as far out of the picture as possible—none of this "Reader, I married him!" business.

Elmore Leonard says that he leaves out of his stories any fancy similes and metaphors and words like "suddenly" and anything that reminds the reader that there is a puppeteer behind the scenes manipulating the strings of the author's marionettes.

> ❝Nowadays the tendency is for the author to stay as far out of the picture as possible....❞

He would not approve of the appropriate but slow start of Anthony Trollope's 1875 novel, *The Way We Live Now*, which begins like this:

> Let the reader be introduced to Lady Carbury, upon whose character and doings much will depend of whatever interest these pages may have, as she sits at her writing-table in her own room in her own house in Welbeck Street. Lady Carbury spent many hours at her desk, and wrote many letters, —wrote also very much besides letters. She spoke of herself in these days as a woman devoted to Literature, always spelling the word with a

big L. Something of the nature of her devotion may be learned by the perusal of three letters which on this morning she had written with a quickly running hand. Lady Carbury was rapid in everything, and in nothing more rapid than in the writing of letters.

A rather pedestrian beginning to one of the best English novels ever written.

And how would Trollope, who was writing in a realistic style ahead of his time, feel about Jay McInerney's 1988 novel, *Story of My Life*?

Here is how he begins this very modern novel, and we can almost hear the narrator telling her tale:

I'm like, I don't believe this shit.

I'm totally pissed at my old man who's somewhere in the Virgin Islands, I don't know where. The check wasn't in the mailbox today which means I can't go to school Monday morning. I'm on the monthly payment program because Dad says wanting to be an actress is some flaky whim and I never stick to anything—this from a guy who's been married five times—and this way if I drop out in the middle of the semester he won't get burned for the full tuition. Meanwhile he buys his new bimbo Tanya who's a year younger than me a 450 SL convertible— always gone for the young ones, haven't we, Dad?—plus her own condo so she can have some privacy to do her writing. Like she can even *read*. He actually believes her when she says she's writing a novel but when I want to spend eight hours a day busting ass at Lee Strasberg it's like, *another one of Alison's crazy ideas*. Story of my life. My old man is fifty-two going on twelve. And then there's Skip Pendleton, which is another reason I'm pissed.

So I'm on the phone screaming at my father's secretary when there's a call on my other line. I go hello and this guy goes, hi, I'm whatever-his-name-is, I'm a friend of Skip's and I say yeah? And he says, I thought maybe we could go out some time.

And I say, what am I, dial-a-date.

Skip Pendleton's this jerk I was in lust with once for about three minutes. He hasn't called me in like three weeks which is fine, okay. I can deal with that, but suddenly I'm like a baseball card he trades with his friends? Give me a break. So I go to this guy, what makes you think I'd want to go out with you, I don't even know you and he says, Skip told me about you. Right. So I'm like, what did he tell you? And the guy goes—Skip said you were hot. I say, great, I'm totally honored that the great Skip Pendleton thinks I'm hot. I'm just a jalapeño pepper waiting for some strange burrito, honey. I mean, *really*.

And this guy says to me, we were sitting around at Skip's place about five in the morning the other night wired out of our minds and I say—this is the guy talking—I wish we had some women and Skip is like, I could always call Alison, she'd be over like a shot.

He said that? I say. I can hear his voice exactly, it's not like I'm totally amazed, but still I can't believe even *he* would be such a pig and suddenly I feel like a cheap slut and I want to scream at this asshole but instead I say, where are you? He's on West Eighty-ninth, it figures, so I give him an address on Avenue C, a rathole where a friend of mine lived last year until her place was broken into for the seventeenth time and which is about as far away from the Upper West Side as you can get without crossing water, so I tell him to meet me there in an hour and at least I have the satisfaction of thinking of him spending about twenty bucks for a cab and then hanging around the doorway of this tenement and maybe getting beat up by some drug dealers....

It sounds real, we believe it, and we learn so much about this character by the voice in the prose.

Way back in 1719, Daniel Defoe tried to con readers into thinking his novel, *The Life and Adventures of Robinson Crusoe*, was based on an actual journal, writing in the preface: "The Editor believes the thing to be a just History of Fact; neither is there any Appearance of Fiction in it." But, of course, Defoe was not the editor of a journal kept by a man named Crusoe; there was no journal, but at the time many readers believed it was all true. Defoe got the basic idea by reading of a sailor, Alexander Selkirk, who was marooned for four years and four months on an island off the coast of Chile. Defoe expanded the time; for example, Robinson doesn't meet the fictional Friday until he has been alone on the island for twenty-four years.

Thomas Mann begins his story "Railway Accident" in a "this-really-happened" manner. You are made to believe from the start that this happened, though, of course, it is fiction.

> Tell you a story? But I don't know any. Well, yes, after all, here is something I might tell.

Mann doesn't sound very excited about the story he's about to tell.

> Once, two years ago now it is, I was in a railway accident; all the details are clear in my memory.
>
> It was not really a first-class one—no wholesale telescoping or "heaps of unidentifiable dead"—not that sort of thing. Still, it was a proper accident, with all the trimmings, and on top of that it was at night. Not everybody has been through one, so I will describe it the best I can.
>
> I was on my way to Dresden, whither I had been invited by some friends of letters: it was a literary and artistic pilgrimage, in short, such as, from time to time, I undertake not unwillingly. You make appearances, you attend functions, you show yourself to admiring crowds—not for nothing is one a subject of William II. And certainly Dresden is beautiful, especially the Zwinger; and afterwards I intended to go for ten days or a fortnight to the White Hart to rest, and if, thanks to the treatments, the spirit should come upon me, I might do a little work as well. To this end I had put my manuscript at the bottom of my trunk, together with my notes—a good stout bundle done up in brown paper and tied with string in the Bavarian colours. I like to travel in comfort, especially when my expenses are paid. So I patronized the sleeping-cars, reserving a place days ahead in a first-class compartment. All was in order; nevertheless I was excited, as I always am on such occasions, for a journey is still an adventure to me, and where traveling is concerned I shall never manage to feel properly blasé.

Unfortunately, the accident is indeed a "not really first-class one" and the story doesn't live up to our idea of "an exciting accident story," proving that even great writers like Mann can write a dud. As Sinclair Lewis once said to me: "Y'know we writers have a gift most normal people don't have—we can bore people long after we're dead."

John Cheever begins his short story, "The Ocean," irresistibly, confiding only to his journal (and to us, the readers):

> I am keeping this journal because I believe myself to be in some danger and because I have no other way of recording my fears. I cannot report them to the police, as you will see, and I cannot confide in my friends. The losses I have recently suffered in self-esteem, reasonableness, and charity are conspicuous, but there is always some painful ambiguity about who is to blame. I might be to blame myself. Let me give you an example. Last night I sat down to dinner with Cora, my wife, at half past six. Our only daughter has left home, and we eat, these days, in the kitchen, off a table ornamented with a goldfish bowl. The meal was cold ham, salad, and potatoes. When I took a mouthful of salad I had to spit it out. "Ah, yes," my wife said. "I was afraid that would happen. You left your lighter fluid in the pantry, and I mistook it for vinegar."
>
> As I say, who was to blame? I have always been careful about putting things in their places and had she meant to poison me she wouldn't have done anything so clumsy as to put lighter fluid in the salad dressing.

She wouldn't? We must read on eagerly, and a little fearfully.

ଚ ❖ ଓ

Neil Simon once told me that if ever he wanted to bring the entire audience up short, to have them leaning forward in their seats in anticipation, he only had to have one character say to the other in so many words:

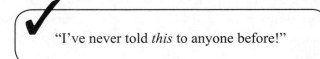

"I've never told *this* to anyone before!"

Edgar Rice Burroughs learned the trick even before Neil Simon. His *Tarzan of the Apes* begins:

> I heard this story from one who had no business to tell it to me, or to any other....

Wow! He's going to tell us a story almost nobody's ever heard! We lean forward in our seats.

A terrible writer, Burroughs was a great storyteller, and he created a perennial icon in his hero, Tarzan, who, seemingly, will never die. (Tarzan, however, owes his genesis to Rudyard Kipling's Mowgli in *The Jungle Book*, which also appears to be ageless, and, is indisputably much better written!)

Burroughs was given to phrases like (and I'm not making it up) "the "great ape was carrying Jane off to a fate worse than death!" However, his descriptions of action were excellent.

Erica Jong begins her *seemingly* very frank and semi-autobiographical novel *Fear of Flying* like this:

> There were 117 psychologists on the PanAm flight to Vienna, and I'd been treated by at least six of them.

It would be easy to dismiss this lead as grandstanding, but it actually is quite a remarkable accomplishment. Look what she succeeds in doing in one sentence:

We know where we are.

We know that we have a protagonist who is troubled, *very* troubled.

Plus we know geographically where we are going; Freud lived in Vienna, the Mecca for psychoanalysts, so we might guess this novel will be about sex. Pretty good for just two dozen or so words.

Kurt Vonnegut sneakily lures us into *Slaughterhouse-Five* by pretending to be totally honest:

> All this happened, more or less.

And in the same vein, we have Christina Schwarz's first sentence from her novel, *Drowning Ruth*:

> I suppose people will say it was my fault, that if I'd not gone home that March in 1919, Mathilda, my only sister, would not be dead.

And, consider Kaye Gibbons' first line of *Ellen Foster*:

> When I was little I would think of ways to kill my daddy.

Elizabeth Berg's intimate and folksy introduction to her novel, *Durable Goods,* goes:

> Well, I have broken the toilet.

How dare she begin a book this way! What's it about, for gosh sake?! Got to read on!

This first-person style of creating an opening was very popular in the magazine stories of the 30s and 40s. Here's one from a 1935 issue of *Story Magazine*, a publication that launched many a fine young writer; the story is "That's What Happened to Me" by Michael Fessier:

> **❝How dare she begin a book that way! What's it about, for gosh sake?! Got to read on!❞**

> I have done things and had things happen to me and nobody knows about it. So I am writing about it so that people will know.

Where is this story *going*? I'll give it another couple of sentences at least.

Ford Madox Ford comes right out and tells the reader in his classic novel, *The Good Soldier*:

> This is the saddest story I have ever heard.

In real life, we don't necessarily like sad stories; in books and stories we *gravitate* to them.

Everyone has encountered a chatty, friendly barber; here is Ring Lardner's in his famous story, "Haircut," and naturally he wants to tell us a story—he *insists* on telling us a story! And we are trapped in a barber chair (luckily, it turns out to be a pretty good story)!

> I got another barber that comes over from Carterville and helps me out Saturdays, but the rest of the time I can get along all right alone. You can see for yourself that this ain't no New York City and besides that, the most of the boys works all day and don't have no leisure to drop in here and get themselves prettied up.
>
> You're a newcomer, ain't you? I thought I hadn't seen you round before. I hope you like it good enough to stay. As I say, we ain't no New York City or Chicago, but we have pretty good times. Not as good, though, since Jim Kendall got killed. When he was alive, him and Hod Meyers used to keep this town in an uproar. I bet they was more laughin' done here than any town its size in America.

As a writer, O. Henry was unable to stay *out* of his stories; witness "The Gift of the Magi," the second most famous Christmas story after Dickens' "A Christmas Carol." He constantly intrudes, which tends to date the beloved story.

> One dollar and eighty-seven cents. That was all. And sixty cents of it was in pennies. Pennies saved one and two at a time by bulldozing the grocer and the vegetable man and the butcher until one's cheeks burned with the silent imputation of parsimony that such close dealing implied. Three times Della counted it. One dollar and eighty-seven cents. And the next day would be Christmas.
>
> There was clearly nothing to do but flop down on the shabby little couch and howl. So Della did it. Which instigates the moral reflection that life is made up of sobs, sniffles, and smiles, with sniffles predominating.
>
> While the mistress of the home is gradually subsiding from the first stage to the second, take a look at the home. A furnished flat at $8 per week. It did not exactly beggar description,

but it certainly had that word on the lookout for the mendicancy squad.

(Before you get into the math of that first confusing sentence, you have to remember that in those days, there was a two-cent coin.)

Throughout the story O. Henry injects chatty lines like "Take a look at the home," which reminds us that a writer is at work here. Elmore Leonard's great rule is:

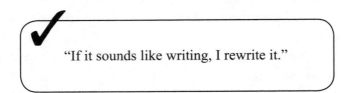

"If it sounds like writing, I rewrite it."

I resisted putting an exclamation point at the ending of Elmore's sentence. "That's the author telling the reader what to think," he would have added. Sentences like "Then he killed her," don't need an exclamation point.

As F. Scott Fitzgerald once said, "using an exclamation point is like laughing at your own joke."

ഇ ❖ ര

Many, *many* stories began with a variation of "I was told this story, which I at first didn't believe, by—", etc. etc. And it's not all *that* bad a way to begin—depending upon your story!

Here are some examples that certainly worked for their famous authors.

Robert Louis Stevenson begins his *Treasure Island* as follows:

> Squire Trelawney, Dr. Livesey, and the rest of these gentlemen having asked me to write down the whole particulars about Treasure Island, from the beginning to the end, keeping nothing back but the bearings of the island, and that only because there is still treasure not yet lifted, I take up my pen in the year of grace 17--, and go back to the time when my father kept the 'Admiral

Benbow' inn, and the brown old seaman, with the saber cut, first took up his lodging under our roof.

I remember him as if it were yesterday, as he came plodding to the inn door, his sea-chest following behind him in a hand-barrow; a tall, strong, heavy, nut-brown man; his tarry pigtail falling over the shoulders of his soiled blue coat; his hands ragged and scarred, with black, broken nails; and the saber cut across one cheek, a dirty, livid white. I remember him looking round the cove and whistling to himself as he did so, and then breaking out in that old sea-song that he sang so often afterwards:--

'Fifteen men on the dead man's chest—
Yo-ho-ho, and a bottle of rum!'

in the high, old tottering voice that seemed to have been tuned and broken at the capstan bars. Then he rapped on the door with a bit of stick like a handspike that he carried, and when my father appeared, called roughly for a glass of rum.

Look how quickly the author gets to a character and a story after telling us why he is writing this!

And the same is true with Edith Wharton's classic novel of 1911, *Ethan Frome*:

I had this story, bit by bit, from various people, and, as generally happens in such cases, each time it was a different story.

And this from the opening of Frank Harris' short story "Montes the Matador."

Yes, I'm better, and the doctor tells me I've escaped once more—as if I cared! ... And all through the fever you came every day to see me, so my niece says, and brought me the cool drink that drove the heat away and gave me sleep. You thought, I suppose, like the doctor, that I'd escape you, too. Ha! Ha! And that you'd never hear old Montes tell what he knows of bull-fighting and you don't.... Or perhaps it was kindness; though why you, a foreigner and a heretic, should be kind to me, God knows.... The doctor says I've not got much more life in me, and you're going to leave Spain within the week—within the week, you said, didn't you? ... Well, then, I don't mind telling you the story.

Thirty years ago I wanted to tell it often enough, but I knew no one I could trust. After that fit passed, I said to myself I'd never tell it; but as you're going away, I'll tell it to you, if you swear by the Virgin you'll never tell it to anyone, at least until I'm dead.

The name of the mythical place, Shangri-La, was created by James Hilton in his huge selling novel of the thirties, *Lost Horizon*. It begins chummily in a men's club:

> Cigars had burned low, and we were beginning to sample the disillusionment that usually afflicts old school friends who have met again as men and found themselves with less in common than they had believed they had.

And then the story of the paradisiacal community unfolds and the reader suspends his disbelief because of the author's skill at convincing us that at first he too was skeptical but that this really could have happened.

Consider still another "storyteller" approach, this from Henry James' 1898 metaphysical thriller, *The Turn of the Screw*:

> The story had held us, round the fire, sufficiently breathless, but except the obvious remark that it was gruesome, as on Christmas Eve in an old house a strange tale should essentially be, I remember no comment uttered till somebody happened to note it as the only case he had met in which such a visitation had fallen on a child.

Italo Calvino's novel, *If on a Winter's Night a Traveler*, begins disarmingly exposed as, well, a novel:

> You are about to begin reading Italo Calvino's new novel, *If on a winter's night a traveler*.

Again, a subjective autobiographical type of beginning; this is from the start of a Ben Hecht story called "The Fabulous Laundryman:"

> I will write this story out as it was told to me, with the hope that you will believe it as did I listening to the bibulous and rococo verbiage of Mr. Dick McCarey.
>
> In the days when I was a newspaper man such a tale as my friend McCarey unleashed between his first and fifteenth drinks in that buzzing Harlem speakeasy would have sent me bouncing into the night to run it down; nor would I have rested till the last detail had been garnered and verified and the whole thing blazoned across a front page. (A statement, this, which such of my erstwhile editors as happen upon these words may very likely challenge with snorts. But what newspaper man, having quit that daft profession, but remembers himself as one of its heroes? And this is not so much a boast as an obeisance to a lost and glamorous vocation.) The bravoes of the press today seem to me a less gaudy lot than those I once knew as colleagues. This McCarey, however, who will in a moment take the floor, is of that species which rather egotistically I choose to fancy extinct. He is of that tribe that once practiced journalism as if it were holy orders.

Damon Runyon, the author of "Guys and Dolls" starts out his short story "Undertaker Song" in typical "damonrunyonese." There's no mistaking the voice:

> Now this story I am going to tell you is about the game of football, a very healthy pastime for the young, and a great character-builder from all I hear, but to get around to this game of football I am compelled to bring in some most obnoxious characters, beginning with a guy by the name of Joey Perhaps, and all I can conscientiously say about Joey is you can have him.
>
> It is a matter of maybe four years since I see this Joey Perhaps until I notice him on a train going to Boston, Mass., one Friday afternoon. He is sitting across from me in the dining-car, where I am enjoying a small portion of baked beans and

brown bread, and he looks over to me once, but he does not rap to me.

There is no doubt but what Joey Perhaps is bad company, because the last I hear of him he is hollering copper on a guy by the name of Jack Ortega, and as a consequence of Joey Perhaps hollering copper, this Jack Ortega is taken to the city of Ossining, N. Y., and placed in an electric chair, and given a very, very, very severe shock in the seat of his pants.

It is something about plugging a most legitimate business guy in the city of Rochester, N. Y., when Joey Perhaps and Jack Ortega are engaged together in a little enterprise to shake the guy down, but the details of this transaction are dull, and sordid, and quite uninteresting, except that Joey Perhaps turns state's evidence and announces that Jack Ortega fires the shot which cools the legitimate guy off, for which service he is rewarded with only a small stretch.

೫ ❖ ೦౩

To end this chapter, let us consider how *War and Peace* begins. This is the novel that *everyone* says is the greatest novel ever written. Does it begin with some high-blown moralization, or a Biblical quotation, or a description of the Russian steppes?

No! Tolstoy was too good a storyteller.

It begins with a chatty introduction:

"Well, prince, Genoa and Lucca are now no more than private estates of the Bonaparte family. No, I warn you, that if you do not tell me we are at war, if you again allow yourself to palliate all the infamies and atrocities of this Antichrist (upon my word, I believe he is), I don't know you in future, you are no longer my friend, no longer my faithful slave, as you say. There, how do you do, how do you do? I see I'm scaring you, sit down and talk to me."

These words were uttered in July 1805 by Anna Pavlovna Scherrer, a distinguished lady of the court, and confidential maid-of-honor to the Empress Mariya Fyodorovna. It was her greeting to Prince Vassily, a man high in rank and office, who was the first to arrive at her *soirée*. Anna Pavlovna had been coughing for the last few days; she had an attack of *la grippe*, as she said—*grippe* was then a new word only used by a few people. In the notes she had sent round in the morning by a footman in red livery, she had written to all indiscriminately:

"If you have nothing better to do, count (or prince), and if the prospect of spending an evening with a poor invalid is not too alarming to you, I shall be charmed to see you at my house between 7 and 10. Annette Scherer."

"Heavens! what a violent outburst!" the prince responded,

....

I don't have to point out how much information and characterization and—a subtle suggestion of conflict------------yes—

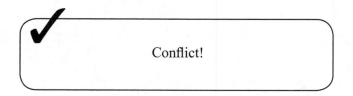

Conflict!

we get right off the bat.

But! Would an editor of today be grabbed or even intrigued by this beginning if he or she didn't know the Olympian name of the author?

So, all in all, how do we feel about this style of beginning a story or novel?

Certainly, I would encourage one to go ahead and start with a how-I-came-to-write-this-story—why am I compelled to tell you about why so-and-so did what he did—or why I *must* break my silence about this tale I was forbidden to ever divulge—and all the other ways there are to seemingly break the barriers between a creator of fiction and seduce the reader-client.

It might very well intrigue the reader, and it also might lend veracity in his or her mind to the many fanciful or realistic events you are about to relate.

But let's take a tip from E.A. Poe, Robert Louis Stevenson, Mark Twain, John Grisham, and all the other great storytellers: After the brief teaser, the nostalgia, the clever first sentence, the come-on, the preview-of-coming-attractions, the *whatever*—get to a scene! Get to some adversarial dialogue, get to some action, get to a troubled, interesting or endangered character.

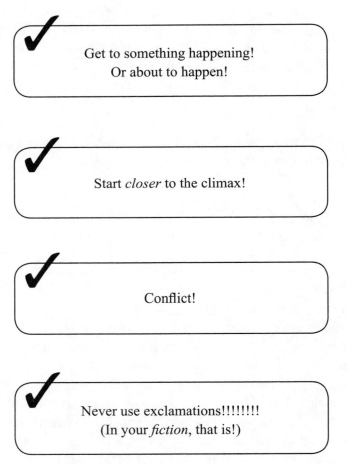

Get to something happening!
Or about to happen!

Start *closer* to the climax!

Conflict!

Never use exclamations!!!!!!!!
(In your *fiction*, that is!)

10

Action

As *in medias res*, this way of starting a story plunges the reader into the middle of things, but usually with vivid *physical* action of some sort. It is often, though not necessarily, violent.

A great example of the purely action beginning is that of Annie Proulx's 1999 short story, "The Mud Below:"

> Rodeo night in a hot little Okie town and Diamond Felts was inside a metal chute a long way from the scratch on Wyoming dirt he named as home, sitting on the back of bull 82N, a loose-skinned brindle Brahma-cross identified in the program as Little Kisses. There was a sultry feeling of weather. He kept his butt cocked to one side, his feet up on the chute rails so the bull couldn't grind his leg, brad him up, so that if it thrashed he could get over the top in a hurry. The time came closer and he slapped his face forcefully, bringing the adrenaline roses up on his cheeks, glanced down at his pullers and said, "I guess." Rito, neck gleaming with sweat, caught the free end of the bull-rope with a metal hook, brought it delicately to his hand from under the bull's belly, climbed up the rails and pulled it taut.
>
> "Aw, this's a sumbuck," he said. "Give you the sample card."
>
> Diamond took the end, made his wrap, brought the rope around the back of his hand and over the palm a second time, wove it between his third and fourth fingers, pounded the rosined glove fingers down over it and into his palm. He laid the tail of the rope across the bull's back and looped the excess, but

it wasn't right—everything had gone a little slack. He undid the wrap and started over, making the loop smaller, waiting while they pulled again and in the arena a clown fired a pink cannon, the fizzing discharge diminished by a deep stir of thunder from the south, Texas T-storm on the roll.

Night perfs had their own hot charge, the glare, the stiff-legged parade of cowboy dolls in sparkle-fringed chaps into the arena, the spotlight that bucked over the squinting contestants and the half-roostered crowd. They were at the end of the night now, into the bullriding, with one in front of him. The bull beneath him breathed, shifted roughly. A hand, fingers outstretched, came across his right shoulder and against his chest, steadying him. He did not know why a bracing hand eased his chronic anxiety. But in the way these things go, that was when he needed twist, to auger him through the ride.

The announcer's galvanized voice rattled in the speakers above the enclosed arena. "Now folks, it ain't the Constitution or the Bill a Rights that made this a great country. It was *God* who created the mountains and plains and the evening sunset and put us here and let us look at them. Amen and God bless the Markin flag. And right now we got a bullrider from Redsled, Wyomin, twenty-three-year-old Diamond Felts, who might be wonderin if he'll ever see that beautiful scenery again. Folks, Diamond Felts weighs one hundred and thirty pounds. Little Kisses weighs two thousand ten pounds, he is a big, big bull and he is thirty-eight and one, last year's Dodge City Bullriders' choice. Only one man has stayed on this big bad bull's back for eight seconds and that was Marty Casebolt at Reno, and you better believe that man got all the money. *Will* he be rode tonight? Folks, we're goin a find out in just a minute, soon as our cowboy's ready. And listen at that rain, folks, let's give thanks we're in a enclosed arena or it would be deep mud below."

Diamond glanced back at the flank man, moved up on his rope, nodded, jerking his head up and down rapidly. "Let's go, let's go."

The chute door swung open and the bull squatted, leaped into the waiting silence and a paroxysm of twists, belly-rolls

and spins, skipping, bucking and whirling, powerful drop, gave
him the menu.

This is an unusual story beginning, which is readily apparent. The
action revolves totally around a man's preparation to ride a bull. We
know nothing of the man's character or why the riding of this bull is
important. We don't even know his age or anything about his appearance
until we hear from the announcer. Later, we get motivations and details
of his appearance, but otherwise we get pure action. One of the reasons
we are interested in the story is the fact that the author truly understands
the intricate techniques of bullriding—and the recondite vocabulary of
the sport.

The action can be grim, like the opening of James Baldwin's 1979
novel, *Just Above My Head*:

> The damn'd blood burst, first through his nostrils, then
> pounded through the veins in his neck, the scarlet torrent ex-
> ploded through his mouth, it reached his eyes and blinded him,
> and brought Arthur down, down, down, down, down.

What's going on? Who knows? We have to find out.

The action can be comic, like Christopher Buckley's opening to his
novel, *No Way to Treat a First Lady*:

> Babette Van Anka had made love to the president of the
> United States on eleven previous occasions, but she still couldn't
> resist inserting "Mr. President" into "Oh, baby, baby, baby." He
> had told her on the previous occasions that he did not like being
> called this while, as he put it, congress was in session.

Buckley then gives us a steamy two-page description of the version
of "Congress in session" which takes place in the Lincoln Bedroom down
the hall from where the First Lady is sleeping. Then:

> Elizabeth Tyler McMann, First Lady of the United States,
> lay awake in her own still-crisp sheets, looking out the window
> toward the Washington Monument. Being married to America's
> most prominent symbol of virility, she was not blind to the

irony of finding herself in bed alone, staring at the nation's most prominent phallic symbol. Not much had ever been lost on Beth McMann, other than happiness.

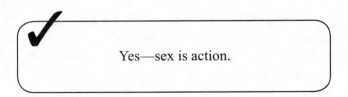

Yes—sex is action.

Witness Anthony Burgess's compelling and outrageous beginning to his novel *Earthly Powers*:

> It was the afternoon of my eighty-first birthday, and I was in bed with my catamite when Ali announced that the archbishop had come to see me.

What—we must continue reading to find out—is going to happen when the archbishop enters the house?

Beginning writers are constantly being preached to (in how-to books) about what makes a satisfactory fictional reading experience.

"The Five C's," which are, or are variations of, "Characters, Conflict, Choice, Change, and Compassion."

But I think one of the important and overlooked letters in The Five C's sermon is the sixth and last one: "S."

For me, it stands for

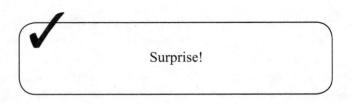

Surprise!

Can you show me a great short story that doesn't revolve around *something surprising*? Or a novel that doesn't have *multiple* surprises?

Weren't you surprised at the end of *Gone with the Wind* when the now-clichéd "Frankly my dear" line was delivered to a—surprised—Scarlett? Or when John Grisham's worthy and modest protagonists lost their valiant fight against the bad guys in his 2008 best-seller, *The Appeal*—with the jury's *surprise* decision?

So even if your beginning is "action-packed," as the blurbs on the dust jackets might assure us, or titillatingly sexy, unless

> **"Can you show me a great short story that doesn't revolve around *something surprising*?"**

there is a little something more implied, the *promise* of a surprise of some sort, it won't grab us.

F. Scott Fitzgerald wrote:

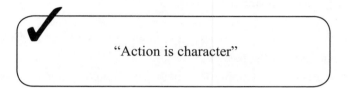

"Action is character"

A perfect example of this can be found in John Cheever's short story, "Montraldo," which begins:

The first time I robbed Tiffany's, it was raining. I bought an imitation-diamond ring at a costume-jewelry place in the Forties. Then I walked up to Tiffany's in the rain and asked to look at rings. The clerk had a haughty manner. I looked at six or eight diamond rings. They began at eight hundred and went up to ten thousand. There was one priced at three thousand that looked to me like the paste in my pocket. I was examining this when an elderly woman—an old customer, I guessed—appeared on the other side of the counter. The clerk rushed over to greet her, and I switched rings. Then I called, "Thank you very much. I'll think it over." "Very well," the clerk said haughtily, and I went out of the store. It was as simple as pie. I walked down to the diamond market in the Forties and sold the ring for eighteen hundred. No questions were asked. Then I went to Thomas Cook and found that the *Conte di Salvini* was sailing for Genoa at five. This was in August, and there was plenty of space on the eastbound crossing. I took a cabin in first class and was standing at the bar when she sailed. The bar was not officially open, of course, but the bar Jack gave me a Martini in a tumbler to hold me until we got into international waters. The *Salvini* had an exceptionally percussive whistle, and you may have heard it if you were anywhere near midtown, although who ever is at five o'clock on an August afternoon?

That night I met Mrs. Winwar and her elderly husband at the horse races. He promptly got seasick, and we plunged into the marvelous skullduggery of illicit love. The passed notes, the phony telephone calls, the affected indifference, and what happened when we were behind the closed door of my cabin made my theft of a ring seem guileless.

Yes, indeed, action is character, and we get a heavy dose of our narrator's character on the first page.

Graham Greene, who wrote sensitively about love and religion, was also a master of the action scene and action beginning. He preferred the word "excitement" rather than action wherever it occurred in a story. He has written about how to write an "excitement" scene:

Excitement is simple: excitement is a situation, a single event. It mustn't be wrapped up in thoughts, similes, metaphors. A simile is a form of reflection, but excitement is of the moment when there is no time to reflect. Action can only be expressed by a subject, a verb, and an object, perhaps a rhythm—little else. Even an adjective slows the pace or tranquilizes the nerve. I should have turned to Stevenson to learn my lesson:

It came all of a sudden when it did, with a rush
of feet and a roar, and then a shout from Alan, and
the sound of blows and someone crying as if hurt.
I looked back over my shoulder and saw Mr. Shuan
in the doorway crossing blades with Alan.

No similes or metaphors there, not even an adjective. But I was too concerned with "the point of view" to be aware of simpler problems, to know that the sort of novel I was trying to write, unlike a poem, was not made with words but with movement, action, character. Discrimination in one's word is certainly required, but not love of one's words....

It is worth reading this passage of Greene's several times.

As to the subject of the adjective, remember Mark Twain's admonition "when in doubt, strike it out."

Movement, action, character....

We have recently read Somerset Maugham's beginning of the unfaithful-wife-caught-in-the-act; let us now look at how Graham Greene handles the same awkward predicament in his beautiful 1951 novel, *The End of the Affair*. The writer Maurice Bendrix and the beautiful Sarah Miles have fallen deeply in love. He goes to her home and finds Henry, his friend and her husband, in bed with a cold. The two lovers cast caution to the wind:

> There was never any question in those days of who wanted whom—we were together in desire. Henry had his tray, sitting up against two pillows in his green woolen dressing-gown, and in the room below, on the hardwood floor, with a single cushion for support and the door ajar, we made love. When the moment came, I had to put my hand gently over her mouth to deaden that strange and angry cry of abandonment, for fear Henry should hear it overhead.
>
> To think I had intended just to pick her brain. I crouched on the floor beside her head and watched and watched, as though I might never see this again—the brown indeterminate-coloured hair like a pool of liquor on the parquet, the sweat on her forehead, the heavy breathing as though she had run a race and now like a young athlete lay in the exhaustion of victory.
>
> And then the stair squeaked. For a moment we neither of us moved. The sandwiches were stacked uneaten on the table, the glasses had not been filled. She said in a whisper, "He went downstairs." She sat in a chair and put a plate in her lap and a glass beside her.
>
> "Suppose he heard," I said, "as he passed."
>
> "He wouldn't have known what it was."
>
> I must have looked incredulous, for she explained with dreary tenderness, "Poor Henry. It's never happened—not in the whole ten years," but all the same we weren't so sure of our

safety; we sat there silently listening until the stair squeaked again. My voice sounded to myself cracked and false as I said rather too loudly. "I'm glad you like that scene with the onions," and Henry pushed open the door and looked in. He was carrying a hot-water-bottle in a grey flannel cover. "Hello, Bendrix," he whispered.

"You shouldn't have fetched that yourself," she said.

"Didn't want to disturb you."

"We were talking about the film last night."

"Hope you've got everything you want," he whispered to me. He took a look at the claret Sarah had put out for me. "Should have given him the '29," he breathed in his unidimensional voice and drifted out again, clasping the hot-water-bottle in its flannel cover, and again we were alone.

Does Henry know? We will keep reading!

The action begins—and ends—with violence in Ambrose Bierce's justly famous Civil War story, "An Occurrence at Owl Creek Bridge."

It begins with a young man, Peyton Farquhar, who is about to be hanged:

> A man stood upon a railroad bridge in northern Alabama, looking down into the swift water twenty feet below. The man's hands were behind his back, the wrists bound with a cord. A rope closely encircled his neck.

Frantically, he thinks of escape, then apparently does break free of the rope and plunges into the river. He avoids the soldiers' bullets and makes it downstream. He finally arrives at his little cottage where his pretty young wife awaits him.

> At the bottom of the steps she stands waiting, with a smile of ineffable joy, an attitude of matchless grace and dignity. Ah, how beautiful she is! He springs forward with extended arms. As he is about to clasp her he feels a stunning blow upon the back of the neck; a blinding white light blazes all about him with a sound like the shock of a cannon—then all is darkness and silence!

Peyton Farquhar was dead; his body, with a broken neck, swung gently from side to side beneath the timbers of the Owl Creek Bridge.

—And the reader realizes with an emotional jolt that the escape was only a split second in the young man's mind. The story is well worth studying, not only for its unique plot, but for Bierce's pithy style and economic, right-on sentences.

Jack London wrote and published some two hundred short stories, as well as many novels, and nearly all of them could be classified as action stories. His 1908 story, "To Build a Fire," is universally acknowledged to be a classic and is said to have been translated into more languages than any work of short fiction in world literature.

I first read it when I was fourteen, and I credit it for turning me on to reading—and then writing. Here are the first simple sentences:

Day had broken cold and grey, exceedingly cold and grey, when the man turned aside from the main Yukon trail and climbed the high earth-bank, where a dim and little-traveled trail led eastward through the fat spruce timberland. It was a steep bank, and he paused for breath at the top, excusing the act to himself by looking at his watch.

We soon learn that the man *must* build a fire or die. It should be easy. It turns out not to be—everything goes wrong, really wrong. It is too great a story to trivialize by telling what happens in a few words. Every would-be writer should read it at least once. It is one of the few great stories ever written with no dialogue; the only other living thing in the story is the man's dog.

There is a great lesson to be learned here; London wrote the story first in 1902 and published it. Here's how that version began:

For land travel or seafaring, the world over, a companion is usually considered desirable. In the Klondike, as Tom Vincent found out, such a companion is absolutely essential. But he found it out, not by precept, but through bitter experience.

"Never travel alone," is a precept of the north. He had heard it many times and laughed; for he was a strapping young fellow, big-boned and big-muscled, with faith in himself and in the strength of his head and hands.

It was on a bleak January day when the experience came that taught him respect for the frost, and for the wisdom of the men who had battled with it.

He had left Calumet Camp on the Yukon with a light pack on his back, to go up Paul Creek to the divide between it and Cherry Creek where his party was prospecting and hunting moose.

This version is totally different in style and tone, and it even ends happily with the man building a fire and surviving! It is not memorable—except that it proves the truism:

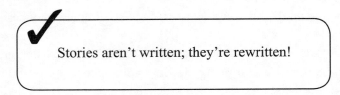

Stories aren't written; they're rewritten!

In the six years between the first and ultimate version of the story, London apparently decided not to begin with a tame generalization, not to bother giving his hero a name, and not to explain where and why he is there in the very beginning.

He simply plunged an unnamed man into a dangerous situation where action was desperately called for.

London was very good at that. Take "Lost Face," a remarkable action story, but lesser known than "To Build a Fire." It is worth taking a good, long look at it. The beginning starts with the end—namely: "It was the end."

This is a brutal story of how a clever man, Subienkow, extricates himself from an impossibly terrible situation by his own determination, guile, bravery, and ingenuity.

It was the end. Subienkow had travelled a long trail of bitterness and horror, homing like a dove for the capitals of Europe, and here, farther away than ever, in Russian America, the trail ceased. He sat in the snow, arms tied behind him, waiting the torture. He stared curiously before him at a huge Cossack, prone in the snow, moaning in his pain. The men had finished handling the giant and turned him over to the women. That they exceeded the fiendishness of the men, the man's cries attested.

Subienkow looked on, and shuddered. He was not afraid to die. He had carried his life too long in his hands, on that weary trail from Warsaw to Nulato, to shudder at mere dying. But he objected to the torture. It offended his soul. And this offense, in turn, was not due to the mere pain he must endure, but to the sorry spectacle the pain would make of him. He knew that he would pray, and beg, and entreat, even as Big Ivan and the others that had gone before. This would not be nice. To pass out bravely and cleanly, with a smile and a jest—ah! That would have been the way. But to lose control, to have his soul upset by the pangs of the flesh, to screech and gibber like an ape, to become the veriest beast—ah, that was what was so terrible.

On a sudden bit of inspiration, Subienkow tells the chief, Makamuk, that he knows how to make a magical potion which, when rubbed on a person's neck, will make it impervious to a sword blow. The chief is skeptical but intrigued.

"When all is ready, I will rub the medicine on my neck, so, and lay my neck there on that log. Then can your strongest hunter take the axe and strike three times on my neck. You yourself can strike the three times."

Makamuk stood with gaping mouth, drinking in this latest and most wonderful magic of the fur-thieves.

"But first," the Pole added hastily, "between each blow I must put on fresh medicine. The axe is heavy and sharp, and I want no mistakes."

"All that you have asked shall be yours," Makamuk cried in a rush of acceptance. "Proceed to make your medicine."

He releases Subienkow in the custody of twenty warriors to go into the forest.

Subienkow did not waste time in gathering the ingredients for his medicine. He selected whatsoever came to hand such as spruce needles, the inner bark of the willow, a strip of birch bark, and a quantity of moss-berries, which he made the hunters dig up for him from beneath the snow. A few frozen roots completed his supply, and he led the way back to camp.

Makamuk and Yakaga crouched beside him, noting the quantities and kinds of the ingredients he dropped into the pot of boiling water.

"You must be careful that the moss-berries go in first," he explained.

"And—oh yes, one other thing—the finger of a man. Here, Yakaga, let me cut off your finger."

But Yakaga put his hands behind him and scowled.

"Just a small finger," Subienkow pleaded.

"Yakaga, give him your finger," Makamuk commanded.

"There be plenty of fingers lying around," Yakaga grunted, indicating the human wreckage in the snow of the scores of persons who had been tortured to death.

"It must be the finger of a live man," the Pole objected.

"Then shall you have the finger of a live man." Yakaga strode over to the Cossack and sliced off a finger.

"He is not yet dead," he announced, flinging the bloody trophy in the snow at the Pole's feet. "Also, it is a good finger, because it is large."

Subienkow dropped it into the fire under the pot and began to sing. It was a French love-song that with great solemnity he sang into the brew.

"Without these words I utter into it, the medicine is worthless," he explained. "The words are the chiefest strength of it. Behold, it is ready."

"Name the words slowly, that I may know them," Makamuk commanded.

"Not until after the test. When the axe flies back three times from my neck, then will I give you the secret of the words."

Subienkow lies down with his head on a log and says to the chief:

"I laugh at you and your strength, O Makamuk," he said. "Strike, and strike hard."

He lifted his hand. Makamuk swung the axe, a broadaxe for the squaring of logs. The bright steel flashed through the frosty air, poised for a perceptible instant above Makamuk's head, then descended upon Subienkow's bare neck. Clear through flesh and bone it cut its way, biting deeply into the log beneath. The amazed savages saw the head bounce a yard away from the blood-spouting trunk.

There was a great bewilderment and silence, while slowly it began to dawn in their minds that there had been no medicine. The fur-thief had outwitted them. Alone, of all their prisoners, he had escaped the torture. That had been the stake for which he played. A great roar of laughter went up. Makamuk bowed his head in shame. The fur-thief had fooled him. He had lost face before all his people. Still they continued to roar out their laughter. Makamuk turned, and with bowed head stalked away. He would be Lost Face; the record of his shame would be with him until he died; and whenever the tribes gathered in the spring for the salmon, or in the summer for the trading, the story would pass back and forth across the camp-fires of how the fur-thief died peaceably, at a single stroke, by the hand of Lost Face.

"Who was Lost Face?" he could hear, in anticipation, some answer, "he who once was Makamuk in the days before he cut off the fur-thief's head."

Even though the protagonist-hero dies at the end of the action, like Sydney Carton in Dickens' *Tale of Two Cities* and Robert Jordan in Hemingway's *For Whom the Bell Tolls*, it is a satisfactory ending because the protagonist has triumphed in his chosen way.

As Shakespeare has Malcolm say in *Macbeth*: "Nothing in his life became him like the leaving it."

11

Epistolary

THIS CATEGORY OF BEGINNINGS, THOUGH WITH A LONG AND honorable history, is used sparingly these days.

Its famous example was created in a 1740 work by Samuel Richardson. It was called *Pamela, or Virtue Rewarded,* a romantic tale of a young servant girl who must dodge many lascivious attempts upon her virginity but who ultimately finds honorable happiness through her goodness. Not only the beginning but the entire novel is told in letters, and it is important only because it is considered to be one of the first romantic novels ever written.

Perhaps Richardson took the idea of epistolary form from Jonathan Swift, who published his famed and enduring *Gulliver's Travels* in 1727, beginning thusly:

A LETTER
From Capt. Gulliver, *to his Cousin* Sympson

I hope you will be ready to own publickly, whenever you shall be called to it, that by your great and frequent Urgency you prevailed on me to publish a very loose and uncorrect Account of my Travels; with Direction to hire some young Gentlemen of either University to put them in Order, and correct the Style, as my Cousin Dampier did by my Advice, in his Book called, A Voyage round the World. But I do not remember I gave you Power to consent, that any thing should be omitted, and much less that any thing should be inserted: Therefore, as to the latter,

I do here renounce every thing of that Kind; particularly a Paragraph about her Majesty the late Queen Anne, of most pious and glorious Memory; although I did reverence and esteem her more than any of human Species. But you, or your Interpolator, ought to have considered, that as it was not my Inclination, so was it not decent to praise any Animal of our Composition before my Master Houyhnhnm: And besides, the Fact was altogether false; for to my Knowledge, being in England during some Part of her Majesty's Reign, she did govern by a chief Minister; nay, even by two successively; the first whereof was the Lord of Godolphin, and the second the Lord of Oxford; so that you have made me say the thing that was not. Likewise, in the Account of the Academy of Projectors, and several Passages of my Discourse to my Master Houyhnhnm, you have either omitted some material Circumstances, or minced or changed them in such a Manner, that I do hardly know mine own Work.

Many people still think of *Gulliver's Travels* as a children's story. I took a three-month college course on that one book and learned what a cynical and scathing political satire it truly is. I remember the professor caustically pointing out that the fierce war the Lilliputians were engaged in was "one of the only two wars in all history where both sides knew exactly what they were fighting about"— first, the Greeks and Trojans fighting for Helen, and second, the Lilliputians fighting their enemy, The Little Enders, over whether it was proper to open a breakfast boiled egg on the big end or the little end.

Many, many stories and novels have begun with a letter, but few have been told entirely with letters in modern times. One, a blockbuster, Pulitzer Prize-winner, and important film, is Alice Walker's *The Color Purple*, written in 1982. The letters are to and from Celi, the protagonist, an uneducated child-wife living in the South, and her adored sister, Nettie, a missionary in Africa. Mostly the letters are from Celie to God, beginning with this:

You better not never tell nobody but God. It'd kill your mammy.

Dear God,

I am fourteen years old. ~~I am~~ I have always been a good girl. Maybe you can give me a sign letting me know what is happening to me.

Last spring after little Lucious come I heard them fussing. He was pulling on her arm. She say It too soon, Fonso, I ain't well. Finally he leave her alone. A week go by, he pulling on her arm again. She say Naw, I ain't gonna. Can't you see I'm already half dead, an all of these children.

> "Many, many stories and novels have begun with a letter, but few have been told entirely with letters in modern times."

She went to visit her sister doctor over Macon. Left me to see after the others. He never had a kine word to say to me. Just say You gonna do what your mammy wouldn't. First he put his thing up gainst my hip and sort of wiggle it around. Then he grab hold my titties. Then he push his thing inside my pussy. When that hurt, I cry. He start to choke me, saying You better shut up and git used to it.

But I don't never git used to it. And now I feels sick every time I be the one to cook. My mama she fuss at me an look at me. She happy, cause he good to her now. But too sick to last long.

The letters are exchanged for some forty years and end with a letter that begins:

Dear God. Dear stars, dear trees, dear sky, dear peoples. Dear Everything. Dear God.

Thank you for bringing my sister Nettie and our children home.

The book is a *tour de force* and incredibly moving.

A perennial favorite novel is Elizabeth Forsythe Hailey's *A Woman of Independent Means*, published in 1978, and re-issued many times.

It begins with the following 1899 letter:

December 10, 1899
Honey Grove, Texas

Dear Rob,

I just asked Miss Appleton to put us on the same team for the spelling bee. Since we're the only two people in the fourth grade who can spell "perspicacious," our team is sure to win.

Can you come over after school? The gardener is clearing the hollyhock bed so there will be more room to play tag. It was my idea.

Bess

Then a few weeks later:

January 2, 1900
Honey Grove

Dear Rob,

Happy New Century! I wish I could live to see a new millennium (if you don't know what that means, I'll tell you after school).

Can you come over today? I'll show you everything I got for Christmas. I got everything I asked for, but I always do.

Bess

Then two years later:

May 30, 1902
Honey Grove

Dear Rob,

Good news! Papa rented his downtown lot to a merry-go-round for the summer. I talked him into taking half the rent in tickets. I'll split my share with you, and we'll ride round and round till time to go back to school.

Bess

Then four years later:

February 8, 1906
Honey Grove

Dear Rob,

This has been the longest winter of my life. I wish my parents would let you come up to my room when you bring my schoolwork, but everyone knows tuberculosis is contagious.

I am sad to think you will be a grade ahead of me in September. To think I am just fifteen and I have already lost a year of my life! Somehow I will make up for it and then I will never lose another day.

Your Bess

Then three years later:

May 1, 1909
Mary Baldwin College
Staunton, Virginia

Dear Rob,

I have seen enough of the world—or at least the world without you. College is fine but just the beginning of all I want to know. I can continue on my own. Next month I am coming home to stay.

I will be in the front row for your graduation. Please don't accept any job offers until I get there.

Ever your
Bess

Then four days later:

May 5, 1909
Staunton

Dearest Mama,

I will be home in a month, and Rob and I will be married this summer. Please don't say anything to him as I want to be the first to tell him.

And, finally, we are off and running!

Notice how quickly we get through the years with a few telling letters and some subtly told information.

The author has said that the letter form "seemed perfectly suited to my character. Letters are a very dramatic device, spanning time, eliminating the need for narrative description, and, most important, enlisting the imagination of the reader to supply the offstage action. I also wanted to write a novel my playwright husband would read. Like most dramatists who are challenged by the strict economy of the stage, he was impatient with prose."

Her novel covers 69 years until the death of the protagonist.

The structure is almost identical to another work written entirely in letters, A.R. Gurney's *Love Letters*, published in 1989.

Love Letters, one of the most successful stage productions ever written, is not technically a play. It is a *tour de force*, merely a man and a woman reading letters from two children who grow up in front of our mental eyes and never cease to write each other—and love each other—until one of their deaths. It begins:

> ANDY: Andrew Makepeace Ladd, the Third, accepts with pleasure the kind invitation of Mr. and Mrs. Gilbert Channing Gardner for a birthday party in honor of their daughter Melissa on April 19th, 1937, at half past three o'clock...

We see them growing up, note by note:

> ANDY: Will you be my valentine?
> MELISSA: Were you the one who sent me a valentine saying "Will you be my valentine?"
> ANDY: Yes I sent it.
> MELISSA: Then I will be. Unless I have to kiss you.

And then, gradually, but suddenly, they show themselves growing up:

> ANDY: Thank you for sending me the cactus plant stuck in the little donkey. I've gotten lots of presents here in the hospital and I have to write thank-you notes for every one. I hate it here. My throat is sore all the time from where they cut

out my tonsils. They give me lots of ice cream, but they also take my temperature the wrong way.

It soon gets serious, and as they grow older, get married (not to each other!) and encounter the many vicissitudes of life, we get to know them very, very well and to know everything about them, and most of all—

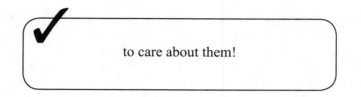

to care about them!

—which is what fiction writing is about. Besides being a very enjoyable read, the aspiring writer can learn a great deal by hearing or reading the entire poignant *Love Letters*. We care about the characters from the beginning because we learn about their little childhood problems—which are not little to *them* and are universal. We suffer through their parents' problems and their teenage problems. We want them to get together—we can see that they truly love each other! But it never happens—which may reinforce the good, suspenseful advice to writers of fiction:

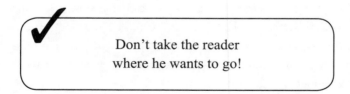

Don't take the reader
where he wants to go!

Though a conventionally written novel, Josephine Humphreys' *Rich in Love* uses a letter early on as a sly device to make the reader immediately like and empathize with the heroine. The girl has come home to find on the desk a letter from her mother to her father. He is outside fishing and hasn't seen or read the letter yet:

I looked away and caught sight of a piece of paper on the hall desk. A note, folded, addressed to him. While he reeled in the fish, I read his note. It had been written on Mother's word processor.

Dear Warren,

I should have discussed this with you in person, but the bus is coming and I have to run, so I will call you when I get settled. This is not just a sudden whim, I have thought it over very carefully. We can get together and talk about it later, but to make a long story short, it is time for me to start a second life. Please tell Lucille.

Helen

He was still standing on the dock, in old khakis and a long-billed cap. He took his fish off the line and put it on a stringer hanging from the dock, then rebaited his hooks. My only thought was how I could soften the blow I held in my hand. Mother's note was hard as a hatchet-chop. Where was the sorrow and the regret? You don't walk out of a twenty-seven-year marriage—or *catch a bus out*—without conveying some sort of emotion to the other person. This note had no feeling. I read the thing again just to make sure I understood it; except for a couple of phrases, it might have been a note saying she was stepping out for a yoga class or a camellia show. But there it said, "start a second life." It said, "when I get settled." There was no doubt about the message. But not a word of pain or guilt. Not a word of explanation. Just those starry gray words off her dot-matrix printer.

Pop had cleaned his hooks and was loading the tackle box. I got a pen and notepad from the desk drawer and wrote another note.

Warren dearest,

I am so confused, absolutely *adrift*, I don't know what to do with my life at this point. After all these years I suddenly discover an emptiness at the heart of things. Please do not blame yourself, Warren, my love. This is something that I have to work out alone. Please forgive me.

> All my love
> Helen

She puts the new note where the old one had been.

> I might not have done this if my father had been a different sort of man. But he was a man with a breakable heart.

How can we not care for such a compassionate and intelligent young girl? With this one scene, the author has made us like two characters, the empathetic girl and the wronged father, and dislike another, the cold mother.

> ✔ Making the reader like or dislike a character
> is more than half the battle of characterization!

So the epistolary form is certainly not dead or even moribund. It has an immediate grabbing interest for a reader—

Hey! We are reading someone's private mail! What are we going to find out—who knows?

But there are difficulties and pitfalls, for example, how to let the readers know what the different characters look like without being too obviously manipulative and showing the author's hand.

12

Emotion

APPEALING IMMEDIATELY TO THE READER'S EMOTION, AIMING FOR the heart, is usually a sure-fire way to begin a story.

> ✓ A child in trouble immediately
>   evokes emotion in people.

Alphonse Daudet knew this when he wrote "The Death of the Dauphin" around 1880. The short story begins:

> The little Dauphin is sick; the little Dauphin is going to die. In all the churches of the realm the Blessed Sacrament is exposed night and day, and tall candles are burning for the recovery of the royal child. The streets in the old residence are sad and silent, the bells no longer ring, and carriages go at a footpace.
>
> About the palace the curious citizens watch, through the iron grilles, the porters with gilt paunches talking in the courtyards with an air of importance.
>
> The whole château is in commotion. Chamberlains, major-domos, run hastily up and down the marble staircases.

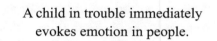

❝Appealing immediately to the reader's emotion, aiming for the heart, is usually a sure-fire way to begin a story.❞

The galleries are full of pages and of courtiers in silk garments, who go from group to group asking news in undertones. On the broad steps weeping maids of honor greet one another with low courtesies, wiping their eyes with pretty embroidered handkerchiefs.

In the orangery there is a great assemblage of long-robed doctors. Through the windows they can be seen flourishing their long black sleeves and bending majestically their hammerlike wigs. The little Dauphin's governor and equerry walk back and forth before the door, awaiting the decision of the faculty. Scullions pass them by without saluting them. The equerry swears like a heathen, the governor recites lines from Horace. And meanwhile, in the direction of the stables one hears a long, plaintive neigh. It is the little Dauphin's horse, calling sadly from his empty manger.

And the king? Where is *monseigneur* the king? The king is all alone in a room at the end of the château. Majesties do not like to be seen weeping. As for the queen, that is a different matter. Seated at the little Dauphin's pillow, her lovely face is bathed in tears, and she sobs aloud before them all, as a linen draper's wife might do.

In his lace-bedecked crib the little Dauphin, whiter than the cushions upon which he lies, is resting now with closed eyes. They think that he sleeps; but no. The little Dauphin is not asleep. He turns to his mother, and seeing that she is weeping, he says to her:

"Madame queen, why do you weep? Is it because you really believe that I am going to die?"

The queen tries to reply. Sobs prevent her from speaking.

"Pray do not weep, madame queen; you forget that I am the Dauphin, and that dauphins cannot die like this."

The queen sobs more bitterly than ever, and the little Dauphin begins to be alarmed.

"I say," he says, "I don't want Death to come and take me and I will find a way to prevent his coming here. Let them send at once forty very strong troopers to stand guard around our bed! Let a hundred big guns watch night and day with matches lighted, under our windows! And woe to Death if it dares approach us!"

To please the royal child the queen makes a sign. In a moment they hear the big guns rumbling through the courtyard; and forty tall troopers, halberds in hand, take their places about the room. They are all old soldiers with gray mustaches. The little Dauphin claps his hands when he sees them. He recognizes one of them and calls him:

"Lorrain! Lorrain!"

The soldier steps forward toward the bed.

"I love you dearly, my old Lorrain. Let me see your big sword. If Death tries to take me you must kill him, won't you?"

"Yes, *monseigneur*," Lorrain replies. And two great tears roll down his bronzed cheeks.

This is a real tearjerker, up to and including the end. But it would not get published today; editors would demand more subtlety and indirect emotion.

A child doesn't need to be sick or dying for the reader to become involved; we will become involved immediately if the child has a problem. ("More?" says Oliver Twist.)

Though not a matter of life and death, a child's first day at a new school *seems* like a matter of life or death to that child. Few people are meaner than children to another child who is in some way "different." Flaubert exploits and explores this idea in his great 1857 novel *Madame Bovary*. It begins not with the young female protagonist but with the fifteen-year-old Charles Bovary whom Emma will one day marry. He is a badly dressed country bumpkin and is wearing a strange homemade hat:

It was our custom, when we came in to class, to throw our hats on the floor, in order to have our hands free. As soon as ever we got inside the door, we 'buzzed' them under the form, against the wall, so as to kick up plenty of dust. That was supposed to be 'the thing'. Whether he failed to notice this manœuvre or whether he was too shy to join in it, it is impossible to say, but when prayers were over he was still nursing his cap. That cap belonged to the composite order of headgear, and in it the heterogeneous characteristics of the busby, the Polish shapska, the bowler, the otterskin toque and the cotton nightcap were simultaneously represented. It was, in short, one of those pathetic objects whose mute unloveliness conveys the infinitely wistful expression we may sometimes note on the face of an idiot. Ovoid in form and stiffened with whalebone, it began with a sort of triple line of sausage-shaped rolls running all round its circumference; next, separated by a red band, came alternate patches of velvet and a rabbit-skin; then a kind of bag or sack which culminated in a stiffened polygon elaborately embroidered, whence, at the end of a long, thin cord, hung a ball made out of gold wire, by way of a tassel. The cap was brand new, and the peak of it all shiny.

"Stand up," said the master.

He stood up; and down went his cap. The whole class began to laugh.

He bent down to recover it. One of the boys next him jogged him with his elbow and knocked it down again. Again he stooped to pick it up.

"You may discard your helmet," said the master, who had a pretty wit.

A shout of laughter from the rest of the class quite put the poor fellow out of countenance, and so flustered was he that he didn't know whether to keep it in his hand, put it on the floor or stick it on his head. He sat down, and deposited it on his knees.

"Stand up," said the master again, "and tell me your name."

In mumbling tones the new boy stammered out something quite unintelligible.

"Again!"

Again came the inarticulate mumble, drowned by the shouts of the class.

"Louder!" rapped out the master sharply; "speak up!"

Whereupon the boy, in desperation, opened his jaws as wide as they would go and, with the full force of his lungs, as though he were hailing somebody at a distance, fired off the word: *Charbovari*.

In an instant the class was in an uproar. The din grew louder and louder, a ceaseless *crescendo* created with piercing yells—they shrieked, they howled, they stamped their feet, bellowing at the top of their voices: *Charbovari! Charbovari!* Then, after a while, the storm began to subside. There would be sporadic outbreaks from time to time, smothered by a terrific effort, or perhaps a titter would fizz along a whole row, or a stifled explosion sputter out here and there, like a half-extinguished fuse.

However, beneath a hail of *impots*, order was gradually restored. The master—who had had it dictated, spelled out and read over to him—had at length succeeded in getting hold of the name of Charles Bovary, and forthwith he ordered the hapless wretch to go and sit on the dunce's stool, immediately below the seat of authority. He started to obey, stopped short and stood hesitating.

"'What are you looking for?" said the master.

"My ca—" began the new boy timidly, casting an anxious glance around him.

An angry shout of "Five hundred lines for the whole class," checked, like the *Quos ego*, a fresh outburst. "Stop your noise, then, will you?" continued the master indignantly, mopping his brow with a handkerchief which he had produced from the interior of his cap. "And you, new boy there, just copy out twenty times the words *ridiculus sum!*"

"There," he went on in a milder tone, "you'll get your cap back all right; no one has stolen it."

Of course, we identify with the hapless new boy immediately, and all through his subsequent trials with the very difficult, mercurial and unlovable Emma, whom he ultimately marries and adores until her early death.

In his monumental autobiographical novel, *Of Human Bondage*, Somerset Maugham wastes no time finding our hearts. In the beginning, his protagonist, Philip Carey, who was born with a club foot, is a very young boy who is awakened by a servant to be taken downstairs. His mother, who has just given birth to a stillborn baby, is herself very ill.

Look how much emotion the author gives us in these scenes in the very first pages:

> The day broke gray and dull. The clouds hung heavily, and there was a rawness in the air that suggested snow. A woman servant came into a room in which a child was sleeping and drew the curtains. She glanced mechanically at the house opposite, a stucco house with a portico, and went to the child's bed.
>
> "Wake up, Philip," she said.
>
> She pulled down the bed-clothes, took him in her arms, and carried him downstairs. He was only half awake.
>
> "Your mother wants you," she said.
>
> She opened the door of a room on the floor below and took the child over to a bed in which a woman was lying. It was his mother. She stretched out her arms, and the child nestled by her side. He did not ask why he had been awakened. The woman kissed his eyes, and with thin, small hands felt the warm body through his white flannel nightgown. She pressed him closer to herself.
>
> "Are you sleepy, darling?" she said.
>
> Her voice was so weak that it seemed to come already from a great distance. The child did not answer, but smiled comfortably. He was very happy in the large, warm bed, with those soft arms about him. He tried to make himself smaller still as he cuddled up against his mother, and he kissed her sleepily. In a moment he closed his eyes and was fast asleep. The doctor came forwards and stood by the bed-side.
>
> "Oh, don't take him away yet," she moaned.
>
> The doctor, without answering, looked at her gravely. Knowing she would not be allowed to keep the child much longer, the woman kissed him again; and she passed her hand down his body till she came to his feet; she held the right foot in her hand and felt the five small toes; and then slowly passed her hand over the left one. She gave a sob.
>
> "What's the matter?" said the doctor. "You're tired."
>
> She shook her head, unable to speak, and the tears rolled down her cheeks. The doctor bent down.
>
> "Let me take him."

She was too weak to resist his wish, and she gave the child up. The doctor handed him back to his nurse.

"You'd better put him back in his own bed."

"Very well, sir."

The little boy, still sleeping, was taken away. His mother sobbed, now broken-heartedly.

"What will happen to him, poor child?"

The monthly nurse tried to quiet her, and presently, from exhaustion, the crying ceased. The doctor walked to a table on the other side of the room, upon which, under a towel, lay the body of a still-born child. He lifted the towel and looked. He was hidden from the bed by a screen, but the woman guessed what he was doing.

"Was it a girl or a boy?" she whispered to the nurse.

"Another boy."

The woman did not answer. In a moment the child's nurse came back. She approached the bed.

"Master Philip never woke up," she said.

There was a pause. Then the doctor felt his patient's pulse once more.

"I don't think there's anything I can do just now," he said. "I'll call again after breakfast."

"I'll show you out, sir," said the child's nurse.

They walked downstairs in silence. In the hall the doctor stopped.

"You've sent for Mrs. Carey's brother-in-law, haven't you?"

"Yes, sir."

"D'you know at what time he'll be here?"

"No, sir, I'm expecting a telegram."

"What about the little boy? I should think he'd be better out of the way."

"Miss Watkin said she'd take him, sir."

"Who's she?"

"She's his godmother, sir. D'you think Mrs. Carey will get over it, sir?"

The doctor shook his head.

II

It was a week later. Philip was sitting on the floor in the drawing-room at Miss Watkin's house in Onslow Gardens. He was an only child and used to amusing himself. The room was frilled with massive furniture, and on each of the sofas were three big cushions. There was a cushion too in each arm-chair. All these he had taken and, with the help of the gilt rout chairs, light and easy to move, had made an elaborate cave in which he could hide himself from the Red Indians who were lurking behind the curtains. He put his ear to the floor and listened to the herd of buffaloes that raced across the prairie. Presently, hearing the door open, he held his breath so that he might not be discovered; but a violent hand pulled away a chair and the cushions fell down.

"You naughty boy, Miss Watkin *will* be cross with you."

"Hulloa, Emma!" he said.

The nurse bent down and kissed him, then began to shake out the cushions, and put them back in their places.

"Am I to come home?" he asked.

"Yes, I've come to fetch you."

"You've got a new dress on."

It was in eighteen-eighty-five, and she wore a bustle. Her gown was of black velvet, with tight sleeves and sloping shoulders, and the skirt had three large flounces. She wore a black bonnet with velvet strings. She hesitated. The question she had expected did not come, and so she could not give the answer she had prepared.

"Aren't you going to ask how your mamma is?" she said at length.

"Oh, I forgot. How is mamma?"

Now she was ready.

"Your mamma is quite well and happy."

"Oh, I am glad."

"Your mamma's gone away. You won't ever see her any more."

Philip did not know what she meant.

"Why not?"

"Your mamma's in heaven."

She began to cry, and Philip, though he did not quite understand, cried too.

What is going to happen to this poor little orphaned boy? We will find out when we read the rest of this long and fascinating masterpiece. He is in big trouble—and—

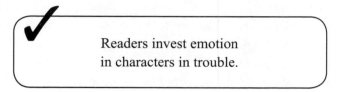

Readers invest emotion
in characters in trouble.

As a playwright—he once had four plays on Broadway at one time—Maugham related his hundreds of short stories and dozens of novels not by telling them but by *showing* them in scene after dramatic scene.

80 ❖ ⊂୧

Death, dying, and killing have inspired a great many emotional beginnings.

In the last of John Updike's Rabbit Angstrom books, *Rabbit at Rest*, the author reveals the imminent death of his hero in the very first sentence:

> Standing amid the tan, excited post-Christmas crowd at the Southwest Florida Regional Airport, Rabbit Angstrom had a funny sudden feeling that what he has come to meet, what's floating in unseen about to land, is not his son Nelson and daughter-in-law Pru and their two children but something more ominous and intimately his: his own death, shaped vaguely like an airplane.

Richard North Patterson's recent novel *The Lasko Tangent* begins with a snapper:

> It was the Monday morning before they killed him. I didn't know then that he existed. Or that I would help change that.

Who kills whom and why? Although we don't know—or yet care—about anyone, our curiosity is aroused.

A similar starter is in Harlan Coben's 2006 bestseller, *The Innocent*:

> You never meant to kill him.
>
> Your name is Matt Hunter. You are twenty years old. You grew up in an upper-middle-class suburb in northern New Jersey, not far from Manhattan. You live on the poorer side of town, but it's a pretty wealthy town. Your parents work hard and love you unconditionally. You are a middle child. You have an older brother whom you worship, and a younger sister whom you tolerate.
>
> Like every kid in your town, you grow up worrying about your future and what college you will get into. You work hard enough and get good, if not spectacular, grades. Your average is an A minus. You don't make the top ten percent but you're close. You have decent extracurricular activities, including a stint as treasurer of the school. You are a letterman for both the football and basketball team—good enough to play Division III but not for a financial scholarship. You are a bit of a wiseass and naturally charming. In terms of popularity, you hover right below the top echelon. When you take your SATs, your high scores surprise your guidance counselor.

Because of that first short, punchy sentence you put up with the ho-hum biography that follows.

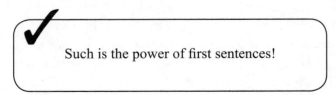

Such is the power of first sentences!

ஐ ❖ ௸

But death and killing aren't the only ways to a reader's emotions.

The great short story writer and playwright, Anton Chekhov, shamelessly plays on our emotions from the start of "The Beggar":

"Kind sir, have pity; turn your attention to a poor, hungry man! For three days I have had nothing to eat; I haven't five kopecks for a lodging. I swear it before God. For eight years I was a village schoolteacher and then I lost my place through intrigues. I fell a victim to calumny. It is a year now since I have had anything to do—"

The advocate Skvortsoff looked at the ragged, fawn-colored overcoat of the applicant, at his dull, drunken eyes, at the red spot on either cheek, and it seemed to him as if he had seen this man somewhere before.

"I have now had an offer of a position in the province of Kaluga," the mendicant went on, "but I haven't the money to get there. Help me kindly; I am ashamed to ask, but—I am obliged to by circumstances."

Skvortsoff's eyes fell on the man's overshoes, one of which was high and the other low, and he suddenly remembered something.

"Look here, it seems to me I met you day before yesterday in Sadovaya Street," he said, "but you told me then that you were a student who had been expelled, and not a village schoolteacher. Do you remember?"

"No-no, that can't be so," mumbled the beggar, taken aback. "I am a village schoolteacher, and if you like I can show you my papers."

"Have done with lying! You called yourself a student and even told me what you had been expelled for. Don't you remember?"

Skvortsoff flushed and turned from the ragged creature with an expression of disgust.

"This is dishonesty, my dear sir!" he cried angrily. "This is swindling! I shall send the police for you, damn you! Even if you are poor and hungry, that does not give you any right to lie brazenly and shamelessly!"

The waif caught hold of the door handle and looked furtively round the antechamber, like a detected thief.

"I—I am not lying—" he muttered. "I can show you my papers."

"Who would believe you?" Skvortsoff continued indignantly.

We, the readers would! Chekhov knew full well that

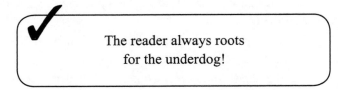

The reader always roots
for the underdog!

Probably the best underdog story I've ever read is John Cheever's "The Five Forty-Eight." It is enormously satisfying, as in the end, the worm turns and the bad guy gets his comeuppance. It begins:

> When Blake stepped out of the elevator, he saw her. A few people, mostly men waiting for girls, stood in the lobby watching the elevator doors. She was among them. As he saw her, her face took on a look of such loathing and purpose that he realized she had been waiting for him.

He, a successful businessman, can't quite remember her name, but he does remember that she had been his secretary for a brief time six months before:

> He saw a dark woman—in her twenties, perhaps—who was slender and shy. Her dress was simple, her figure was not much, one of her stockings was crooked, but her voice was soft and he had been willing to try her out. After she had been working for him a few days, she told him that she had been in the hospital for eight months and that it had been hard after this for her to find work, and she wanted to thank him for giving her a chance. Her hair was dark, her eyes were dark; she left him with a pleasant impression of darkness. As he got to know her better, he felt that she was oversensitive and, as a consequence, lonely. Once, when she was speaking to him of what she imagined his life to be—full of friendships, money, and a large and loving family— he had thought he recognized a peculiar feeling of deprivation. She seemed to imagine the lives of the rest of the world to be

more brilliant than they were. Once, she had put a rose on his desk, and he had dropped it into the wastebasket. "I don't like roses," he told her.

One evening he invites her for a drink and ends up in her shabby apartment:

> She gave him a drink and said that she was going to put on something more comfortable. He urged her to; that was, after all, what he had come for. If he had any qualms, they would have been practical. Her diffidence, the feeling of deprivation in her point of view, promised to protect him from any consequences. Most of the many women he had known had been picked for their lack of self-esteem.

Do we get the feeling that this is not a nice guy?

> When he put on his clothes again, an hour or so later, she was weeping. He felt too contented and warm and sleepy to worry much about her tears. As he was dressing, he noticed on the dresser a note she had written to a cleaning woman. The only light came from the bathroom—the door was ajar—and in this half light the hideously scrawled letters again seemed entirely wrong for her, and as if they must be the handwriting of some other and very gross woman. The next day, he did what he felt was the only sensible thing. When she was out for lunch, he called personnel and asked them to fire her. Then he took the afternoon off. A few days later, she came to the office, asking to see him. He told the switchboard girl not to let her in. He had not seen her again until this evening.

Our blood boils in anger over this guy and our hearts are totally with this fragile girl. Now they are on the train, she having followed him to his commuter train. She sits next to him, tells him he has ruined her life, hasn't been able to get a job since he fired her, and that she has a pistol in her purse leveled at his stomach. He is petrified with fear. But she doesn't shoot him; when they get to his posh destination where his long-suffering wife awaits him, she orders him to a spot away from the station:

When the train had passed beyond the bridge, the noise grew distant, and he heard her screaming at him, "*Kneel down! Kneel down! Do what I say. Kneel down!*"

He got to his knees. He bent his head. "There," she said. "You see, if you do what I say, I won't harm you, because I really don't want to harm you, I want to help you, but when I see your face it sometimes seems to me that I can't help you. Sometimes it seems to me that if I were good and loving and sane—o, much better than I am—sometimes it seems to me that if I were all these things and young and beautiful, too, and if I called to show you the right way, you wouldn't heed me. Oh, I'm better than you, I'm better than you, and I shouldn't waste my time or spoil my life like this. Put your face in the dirt. *Put your face in the dirt!* Do what I say. Put your face in the dirt."

He fell forward in the filth. The coal skinned his face. He stretched out on the ground, weeping. "Now I feel better," she said. "Now I can wash my hands of you, I can wash my hands of all this, because you see there is some kindness, some saneness in me that I can find and use. I can wash my hands." Then he heard her footsteps go away from him, over the rubble.

One of my writing students thought that Blake's punishment was much too light; he wrote an alternate ending in which Miss Dent makes the man take off all his clothes and walk naked back to his comfortable home and life.

This story has much more "body" to it than any précis of it can convey, and I urge every would-be short-story writer to read it.

Here is the beginning to Ring Lardner's much-anthologized short story from the twenties, "Champion," a different type of underdog story:

Midge Kelly scored his first knockout when he was seventeen. The knockee was his brother Connie, three years his junior and a cripple. The purse was a half dollar given to the younger Kelly by a lady whose electric had just missed bumping his soul from his frail little body.

Connie did not know Midge was in the house, else he never would have risked laying the prize on the arm of the least comfortable chair in the room, the better to observe its shining beauty. As Midge entered from the kitchen, the crippled boy covered the coin with his hand, but the movement lacked the speed requisite to escape his brother's quick eye.

"Watcha got there?" demanded Midge.

"Nothin'," said Connie.

"You're a one legged liar!" said Midge.

He strode over to his brother's chair and grasped the hand that concealed the coin.

"Let loose!" he ordered.

Connie began to cry.

"Let loose and shut up your noise," said the elder, and jerked his brother's hand from the chair arm.

The coin fell onto the bare floor. Midge pounced on it. His weak mouth widened in a triumphant smile.

"Nothin', huh?" he said. "All right, if it's nothin' you don't want it."

"Give that back," sobbed the younger.

"I'll give you a red nose, you little sneak! Where'd you steal it?"

"I didn't steal it. It's mine. A lady give it to me after she pretty near hit me with a car."

"It's a crime she missed you," said Midge.

Midge started for the front door. The cripple picked up his crutch, rose from his chair with difficult, and, still sobbing, came toward Midge. The latter heard him and stopped.

"You better stay where you're at," he said.

"I want my money," cried the boy.

"I know what you want," said Midge.

Doubling up the fist that held the half dollar, he landed with all his strength on his brother's mouth. Connie fell to the floor with a thud, the crutch tumbling on top of him. Midge stood beside the prostrate form.

"Is that enough?" he said. "Or do you want this, too?"

And he kicked him in the crippled leg.

"I guess that'll hold you," he said.

There was no response from the boy on the floor. Midge looked at him a moment, then at the coin in his hand, and then went out into the street, whistling.

They say that hate is a much more powerful emotion than love, and the reader certainly hates the character of Midge Kelly from the beginning to the end of this story. We read on, hoping to see the rat get his comeuppance which, unfortunately, he never gets.

Sol Stein, in his wonderful book on writing, *How to Grow a Novel*, says this about violent beginnings:

> In novels that rely on melodrama rather than drama, and particularly in so-called thrillers, readers are now constantly assaulted by someone found dead in paragraph one of chapter one, or a bomb is about to go off, or a killing is about to happen. As the dangers of the real world escalate into acts of terrorism, thriller writers have had to balloon their plots and increase the dangers. But if it is true that the reader must know the people in the car before he sees the car crash, many thrillers don't give us that opportunity. Readers may have some curiosity evoked, but the depth of their emotions is untouched by the kind of clichéd opening that starts with an unmotivated bang to unknown characters. There are notable exceptions. Toni Morrison, winner of the Nobel Prize for literature, starts *Paradise* with "They shoot the white girl first." That's melodrama, but no reader expects Toni Morrison to write a thriller, and they'll gladly wait to find out who the people are.
>
> And so we have a choice. You can begin with a flash fire in the kitchen that endangers the entire house (melodrama), or you put a pot on the boil, bubbling and simmering, as you show your characters acting in a situation that is slowly alarming, a conflict developing into the big event that will hold the reader curious, concerned, perhaps even enthralled, gripped as if glued to your story for its duration.

> ❝We read on, hoping to see the rat get his comeuppance which, unfortunately, he never gets.❞

Anna Quindlen is the author of bestselling novels that draw remarks from reviewers such as "compassionate" and "tender." Her novel *One True Thing* is an example of drawing the reader into the writer's world. The first sentence of the Preface is intriguing: "Jail is not as bad as you might imagine." The reader imagines jail is awful, so he wants to know why the narrator thinks otherwise.

> When I say jail, I don't mean prison. Prison is the kind of place you see in old movies or public television documentaries, those enormous gray places with a guard tower at each corner and curly strips of razor wire going round and round like a loop-the-loop atop the high fence. Prison is where they hit the bars with metal spoons, plan insurrection in the yard, and take the smallest boy—the one in on a first offense—into the shower room, while the guards pretend not to look and leave him to find his own way out, blood trickling palely, crimson mixed with milky white, down the backs of his hairless thighs, the shadows at the backs of his eyes changed forever.
>
> Or at least that's what I've always imagined prison was like.
>
> Jail was not like that a bit, or at least not the jail in Montgomery County. It was two small rooms, both together no bigger than my old attic bedroom in my parents' house, and they did have bars, but they closed by hand, not with the clang of the electric, the remote controlled, the impregnable. An Andy Griffith jail. A Jimmy Stewart jail.

I urge every aspiring writer to read Sol Stein's *How to Grow a Novel*. He expands these thoughts on how to start a novel in an erudite but highly readable manner, being a fine novelist and famous editor himself.

13

The Summing Up

So, IN THIS BOOK WE HAVE NOW SEEN THE TWELVE BASIC WAYS OF starting a story, but look how diverse and varied they are, even within their own categories!

And then, what about the many wonderful beginnings that seem to thumb their nose at being categorized; for example, what to do with Julian Barnes' beginning of his 1991 novel, *Talking It Over*:

> Stuart My name is Stuart, and I remember everything.
> Stuart's my Christian name. My full name is Stuart Hughes. My *full* name: that's all there is to it. No middle name. Hughes was the name of my parents, who were married for twenty-five years. They called me Stuart. I didn't particularly like the name at first—I got called things like Stew and Stew-Pot at school—but I've got used to it. I can handle it. I can handle my handle.
>
> Sorry, I'm not very good at jokes. People have told me that before. Anyway, Stuart Hughes—I think that'll do for me. I don't want to be called St John St John de Vere Knatchbull. My parents were called Hughes. They died, and now I've got their name. And when I die, I'll still be called Stuart Hughes. There aren't too many certainties in this great big world of ours but that's one of them.
>
> Do you see the point I'm making? Sorry, absolutely no reason why you should. I've only just started. You scarcely know me. Let's start again. Hullo, I'm Stuart Hughes, nice to meet you. Shall we shake hands? Right, good. No, the point I'm trying to

make is this: *everyone else around here has changed their name.*
That's quite a thought. It's even a bit creepy.

And Stuart *does* go on. But he's got us hooked by the strangeness
of his beginning.

Now: top honors for *un-categorical* go to the honorable James
Joyce's first paragraphs of his classic *A Portrait of the Artist as a Young
Man*:

> Once upon a time and a very good time it was there was
> a moocow coming down along the road and this moocow that
> was coming down along the road met a nice little boy named
> baby tuckoo....
>
> His father told him that story: his father looked at him
> through a glass: he had a hairy face.
>
> He was a baby tuckoo. The moocow came down the road
> where Betty Byrne lived: she sold lemon platt.
>
> > *O, the wild rose blossoms*
> > *On the little green place.*
>
> He sang that song. That was his song.
>
> > *O, the green wothe botheth.*
>
> When you wet the bed first it is warm then it gets cold. His
> mother put on the oilsheet. That had the queer smell.
>
> His mother had a nicer smell than his father. She played on
> the piano the sailor's hornpipe for him to dance. He danced:
>
> > *Tralala lala*
> > *Tralala tralaladdy*
> > *Tralala lala*
> > *Tralala lala.*

Hoo boy!
And what do we do with the following first line of a story by Eileen
Jensen whose title I've forgotten:

She had slept naked all her life, and no one knew it.

And this metaphysical one by Mildred Cram in her popular novel of yesteryear, *Forever*:

> They met—Colin and Julie—not very long before they were born.

And my own favorite from James Gunn's *Deadlier Than the Male*:

> Helen Brent had the best-looking legs at the inquest.

But to heck with categories—now let's just enjoy a whole bunch of good first sentences—

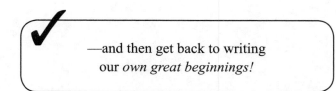

—and then get back to writing our *own great beginnings!*

14

A Potpourri of
Well-Known Beginnings

W HAT FOLLOWS IS A GRAB BAG OF DOZENS OF FIRST SENTENCES,
a laundry list of every type of beginning, in no particular order. Browse
them and determine which might correspond in some way to the beginning of *your* novel or short story.

Do they entice, encourage, or challenge you to want to read the rest
of the work? Some are amusing, some baffling, some chilling—but all
are the beginning of what was a published work and, in many, the start
of a classic and enduring work.

They are worth analyzing.

Ask yourself:

Does this beginning tell, or hint, of something having happened or
about to happen that I might find interesting?

Does it set a scene?

Does it introduce a character of interest?

Does it express "the voice" of the author?

Does it do none of the above, but merely intrigue and invite further
reading?

Read on!

"I wake up afraid. My wife is sitting on the edge of my
bed, shaking me. 'They're at it again,' she says."

Tobias Wolff, *Next Door*

I didn't know their names. I'd never heard their voices. I didn't even know them by sight, strictly speaking, for their faces were too small to fill in with identifiable features at that distance. Yet I could have constructed a timetable of their comings and goings, their daily habits and activities. They were the rear-window dwellers around me.

Cornell Woolrich, *Rear Window*

It was a hard jolt for me, one of the bitterest I ever had to face. And it all came about through my own foolishness, too. Even yet sometimes, when I think of it, I want to cry or swear or kick myself. Perhaps, even now, after all this time, there will be a kind of satisfaction in making myself look cheap by telling of it.

It began at three o'clock one October afternoon as I sat in the grandstand at the fall trotting-and-pacing meet at Sandusky, Ohio.

Sherwood Anderson, *I'm a Fool*

Getting from La Jolla to Alta Vista State Hospital isn't easy, unless you have a car or a breakdown.

Tobias Wolff, *Sanity*

Ours is essentially a tragic age, so we refuse to take it tragically.

D. H. Lawrence, *Lady Chatterly's Lover*

I wish either my father or my mother, or indeed both of them, as they were in duty both equally bound to it, had minded what they were about when they begot me; had they duly considered how much depended upon what they were then doing;—that not only the production of a rational Being was concerned in it, but that possibly the happy formation and temperature of his body, perhaps his genius and the very cast of his mind;—and, for aught they knew to the contrary, even the fortunes of his whole house might take their turn from the humours and dispositions which were then uppermost:—Had they duly weighted and considered all this, and proceeded accordingly,—I am verily persuaded I should have made a quite different figure in the world, from that, in which the reader is likely to see me.

Laurence Sterne, *The Life and Opinions of Tristram Shandy*

Customs of courtship vary greatly in different times and places, but the way the thing happens to be done here and now seems the only natural way to do it.

Herman Wouk, *Marjorie Morningstar*

It was ever of opinion that the honest man who married and brought up a large family did more service than he who continued single, and only talked of population.

Oliver Goldsmith, *The Vicar of Wakefield*

In the ancient city of London, on a certain autumn day in the second quarter of the sixteenth century, a boy was born to a poor family of the name of Canty, who did not want him.

Mark Twain, *The Prince and the Pauper*

"The cow is there," said Ansell, lighting a match and holding it out over the carpet.

E. M. Forster, *The Longest Journey*

"And—and—what comes next?"

Thomas Mann, *Buddenbrooks*

By the time he was nineteen Vance Weston had graduated from the College of Euphoria, Illinois, where his parents then lived, had spent a week in Chicago, invented a new religion, and edited for a few months a college magazine called *Getting There*, to which he had contributed several love poems and a series of iconoclastic essays.

Edith Wharton, *Hudson River Bracketed*

The idea of eternal return is a mysterious one, and Nietzsche has often perplexed other philosophers with it: to think that everything recurs as we once experienced it, and that the recurrence itself recurs ad infinitum!

Milan Kundera, *The Unbearable Lightness of Being*

My name was Salmon, like the fish; first name, Susie. I was fourteen when I was murdered on December 6, 1973. In newspaper photos of missing girls from the seventies, most looked like me: white girls with mousy brown hair. This was before kids of all races and genders started appearing on milk cartons or in the daily mail. It was still back when people believed things like that didn't happen.

Alice Sebold, *The Lovely Bones*

"I have been here before," I said; I had been there before; first with Sebastian more than twenty years ago on a cloudless day in June, when the ditches were white with fool's-parsley and meadowsweet and the air heavy with all the scents of summer; it was a day of peculiar splendour, such as our climate affords once or twice a year, when leaf and flower and bird and sun-lit stone and shadow seem all to proclaim the glory of God; and though I had been there so often, in so many moods, it was to that first visit that my heart returned on this, my latest.

Evelyn Waugh, *Brideshead Revisited*

Riverun, past Eve and Adam's from swerve of share to bend of bay, brings us by a commodius vicus of recirculation back to Howth Castle and Environs.

James Joyce, *Finnegans Wake*

"I see a ring," said Bernard, "hanging above me."

Virginia Woolf, *The Waves*

"To be born again," sang Gibreel Farishta tumbling from the heavens, "first you have to die."

Salman Rushdie, *The Satanic Verses*

So, then people do come here in order to live; I would sooner have thought one died here.

Rainer Maria Rilke, *The Notebooks of Malte Laurids Brigge*

I shall soon be quite dead at last in spite of all.

Samuel Beckett, *Malone Dies*

Once you have given up the ghost, everything follows with dead certainty, even in the midst of chaos.

Henry Miller, *Tropic of Capricorn*

They order, said I, this matter better in France—

Laurence Sterne, *A Sentimental Journey*

I stand at the window of this great house in the south of France as night falls, the night which is leading me to the most terrible morning of my life.

James Baldwin, *Giovanni's Room*

In certain provincial towns there are houses whose appearance arouses a melancholy as great as that of the gloomiest cloisters, the most desolate moorland, or the saddest ruins.

Honoré de Balzac, *Eugénie Grandet*

An easterly is the most disagreeable wind in Lyme Bay—Lyme Bay being that largest bite from the underside of England's outstretched southwestern leg—and a person of curiosity could at once have deduced several strong probabilities about the pair who began to walk down the quay at Lyme Regis, the small but ancient eponym of the inbite, one incisively sharp and blustery morning in the late March of 1867.

John Fowles, *The French Lieutenant's Woman*

A Saturday afternoon in November was approaching the time of twilight, and the vast tract of unenclosed wild known as Egdon Heath embrowned itself moment by moment.

Thomas Hardy, *The Return of the Native*

Now in these dread latter days of the old violent beloved U.S.A. and of the Christ-forgetting Christ-haunted death-dealing Western world I came to myself in a grove of young pines and the question came to me: has it happened at last?

Walker Percy, *Love in the Ruins*

As I walked through the wilderness of this world, I lighted on a certain place, where there was a den; and I laid me down in that place to sleep: and as I slept I dreamed a dream.

John Bunyan, *The Pilgrim's Progress*

For a long time I used to go to bed early.

Marcel Proust, *Swann's Way*

Incredible the first animal that dreamed of another animal.

Carlos Fuentes, *Terra Nostra*

He awoke, opened his eyes.

Paul Bowles, *The Sheltering Sky*

Herman Broder turned over and opened one eye.

Isaac Bashevis Singer, *Enemies, A Love Story*

When the fair gold morning of April stirred Mary Hawley awake, she turned over to her husband and saw him, little fingers pulling a frog mouth at her.

John Steinbeck, *The Winter of Our Discontent*

I think I fell in love with Sally while she was eating breakfast, the first time we were together.

Larry McMurtry, *All My Friends Are Going to Be Strangers*

Often he thought: My life did not begin until I knew her.

Evan S. Connell, *Mr. Bridge*

It was love at first sight.

Joseph Heller, *Catch-22*

It was Wang Lung's marriage day.

Pearl S. Buck, *The Good Earth*

It was inevitable; the scent of bitter almonds always reminded him of the fate of unrequited love.

Gabriel García Márquez, *Love in the Time of Cholera*

Ooow-ow-oow-owow!

Mikhail Bulgakov, *The Heart of a Dog*

Buck did not read the newspapers, or he would have known that trouble was brewing, not alone for himself, but for every tide-water dog, strong of muscle and with warm, long hair, from Puget Sound to San Diego.

Jack London, *The Call of the Wild*

Stately, plump Buck Mulligan came from the stairhead, bearing a bowl of lather on which a mirror and a razor lay crossed.

James Joyce, *Ulysses*

Here is Edward Bear, coming downstairs now, bump, bump, bump, on the back of his head, behind Christopher Robin.

A. A. Milne, *Winnie-the-Pooh*

I have never begun a novel with more misgiving.

W. Somerset Maugham, *The Razor's Edge*

Dr. Weiss, at forty, knew that her life had been ruined by literature.

Anita Brookner, *The Debut*

Shortly after dawn, or what would have been dawn in a normal sky, Mr. Artur Sammler with his bushy eye took in the books and papers of his West Side bedroom and suspected strongly that they were the wrong books, the wrong papers.

Saul Bellow, *Mr. Sammler's Planet*

"You've been reading the wrong books," the business-man said.

V. S. Naipaul, *An Area of Darkness*

Once when I was six years old I saw a magnificent picture in a book, called *True Stories from Nature*, about the primeval forest.

Antoine de Saint-Exupéry, *The Little Prince*

Though I haven't ever been on the screen I was brought up in pictures.

F. Scott Fitzgerald, *The Last Tycoon*

For many years I claimed I could remember things seen at the time of my own birth.

Yukio Mishima, *Confessions of a Mask*

I, Tiberius Claudius Drusus Nero Germanicus This-that-and-the-other (for I shall not trouble you yet with all my titles) who was once, and not so long ago either, known to my friends and relatives and associates as "Claudius the Idiot", or "That Claudius", or "Claudius the Stammerer", or "Clau-Clau-Claudius" or at best as "Poor Uncle Claudius", am now about to write this strange history of my life; starting from my earliest childhood and continuing year by year until I reach the fateful point of change where, some eight years ago, at the age of fifty-one, I suddenly found myself caught in what I may call the "golden predicament" from which I have never since become disentangled.

Robert Graves, *I, Claudius*

Appollon Appollonovich Ableukhov was of venerable stock: he had Adam as his ancestor.

Andrei Bely, *Petersburg*

Felicitas Maria Taylor was called after the one virgin martyr whose name contained some hope for ordinary human happiness.

Mary Gordon, *The Company of Women*

Call me Jonah.

Kurt Vonnegut, Jr., *Cat's Cradle*

I am an American, Chicago born—Chicago, that somber city—and go at things as I have taught myself, free-style, and will make the record in my own way: first to knock, first admitted; sometimes an innocent knock, sometimes a not so innocent.

Saul Bellow, *The Adventures of Augie March*

At the beginning of the summer I had lunch with my father, the gangster, who was in town for the weekend to transact some of his vague business.

Michael Chabon, *The Mysteries of Pittsburgh*

The world is what it is; men who are nothing, who allow themselves to become nothing, have no place in it.

V. S. Naipaul, *A Bend in the River*

Someone must have traduced Joseph K., for without having done anything wrong he was arrested one fine morning.

Franz Kafka, *The Trial*

The door opened to reveal an infinitely spacious room: a whole world of meanings and motivations, not just a limited space buried in a mass of detail.

Naguib Mahfouz, *Respected Sir*

The cell door slammed behind Rubashov.

Arthur Koestler, *Darkness at Noon*

I get the willies when I see closed doors.

Joseph Heller, *Something Happened*

Granted: I am an inmate of a mental hospital; my keeper is watching me, he never lets me out of his sight; there's a peephole in the door, and my keeper's eye is the shade of brown that can never see through a blue-eyed type like me.

Günter Grass, *The Tin Drum*

I am an invisible man.

Ralph Ellison, *Invisible Man*

I am a sick man … I am an angry man.

Fyodor Dostoyevski, *Notes from Underground*

Crude thoughts and fierce forces are my state.

Norman Mailer, *Ancient Evenings*

In eighteenth-century France there lived a man who was one of the most gifted and abominable personages in an era that knew no lack of gifted and abominable personages.

Patrick Süskind, *Perfume*

An author ought to consider himself, not as a gentleman who gives a private or eleemosynary treat, but rather as one who keeps a public ordinary, at which all persons are welcome for their money.

Henry Fielding, *Tom Jones*

One of the most dreadful spectacles we may run across is the malignant aspect of a certain class of the Parisian populace; a class horrible to behold, pallid, yellow, tawny.

Honoré de Balzac, *The Girl with Golden Eyes*

I hate the faces of peasants.

Nadine Gordimer, *A World of Strangers*

In the days when the spinning wheels hummed busily in the farmhouses—and even great ladies, clothed in silk and thread lace, had their toy spinning wheels of polished oak— there might be seen, in districts far away among the lanes, or deep in the bosom of the hills, certain pallid undersized men who, by the side of the brawny country folk, looked like the remnants of a disinherited race.

George Eliot, *Silas Marner*

While the present century was in its teens, and on one sunshiny morning in June, there drove up to the great iron gate of Miss Pinkerton's academy for young ladies, on Chiswick Mall, a large family coach, with two fat horses in blazing harness, driven by a fat coachman in a three-cornered hat and wig, at the rate of four miles an hour.

William Thackeray, *Vanity Fair*

In a village of La Mancha the name of which I don't care to recall, there lived not so long ago one of those gentlemen who always have a lance in the rack, an ancient buckler, a skinny nag, and a greyhound for the chase.

Miguel de Cervantes, *The Adventures of Don Quixote de la Mancha*

All of this happened while I was walking around starving in Christiania—that strange city no one escapes from until it has left its mark on him....

Knut Hamsun, *Hunger*

I am not mad, only old.

May Sarton, *As We Are Now*

One day, I am already old, in the entrance of a public place a man came up to me.

Marguerite Duras, *The Lover*

"What are you doing here, my little man?"

Elias Canetti, *Auto-da-Fé*

You are not the kind of guy who would be at a place like this at this time of the morning.

Jay McInerney, *Bright Lights, Big City*

I can feel the heat closing in, feel them out there making their moves, setting up their devil doll stool pigeons,

crooning over my spoon and dropper I throw away at
Washington Square Station, vault a turnstile and two flights
down the iron stairs, catch an uptown A train ... Young,
good looking, crew cut, Ivy League, advertising exec type
fruit holds the door back for me.

William S. Burroughs, *Naked Lunch*

When Caroline Meeber boarded the afternoon train for
Chicago, her total outfit consisted of a small trunk, a cheap
imitation alligator-skin satchel, a small lunch in a paper box,
and a yellow leather snap purse, containing her ticket, a scrap
of paper with her sister's address in Van Buren Street, and
four dollars in money,

Theodore Dreiser, *Sister Carrie*

Roy Hobbs pawed at the glass before thinking to prick
a match with his thumbnail and hold the spurting flame in
his cupped palm close to the lower berth window, but by then
he had figured it was a tunnel they were passing through and
was no longer surprised at the bright sight of himself holding
a yellow light over his head, peering back in.

Bernard Malamud, *The Natural*

The nickname of the train was the Yellow Dog.

Eudora Welty, *Delta Wedding*

I first heard of Ántonia on what seemed to me
an interminable journey across the great midland plain
of North America.

Willa Cather, *My Ántonia*

To the red country and part of the gray country
of Oklahoma, the last rains came gently, and they did
not cut the scarred earth.

John Steinbeck, *The Grapes of Wrath*

A sharp clip-clop of iron-shod hoofs deadened and
died away, and clouds of yellow dust drifted from under the
cottonwoods out over the sage.

Zane Grey, *Riders of the Purple Sage*

On they went, singing "Rest Eternal," and whenever
they stopped, their feet, the horses, and the gusts of wind
seemed to carry on their singing.

Boris Pasternak, *Doctor Zhivago*

The cold passed reluctantly from the earth, and the retir-
ing fogs revealed an army stretched out on the hills, resting.

Stephen Crane, *The Red Badge of Courage*

It was a feature peculiar to the Colonial wars of North
America, that the toils and dangers of the wilderness were
to be encountered, before the adverse hosts could meet.

James Fenimore Cooper, *The Last of the Mohicans*

An army post in peacetime is a dull place.

Carson McCullers, *Reflections in a Golden Eye*

The huge black clock hand is still at rest but is on the
point of making its once-a-minute gesture; that resilient jolt
will set a whole world in motion.

Vladimir Nabokov, *King, Queen, Knave*

Under certain circumstances there are few hours in life more agreeable than the hour dedicated to the ceremony known as afternoon tea.

Henry James, *The Portrait of a Lady*

One summer afternoon Mrs. Oedipa Maas came home from a Tupperware party whose hostess had put perhaps too much Kirsch in the fondue to find that she, Oedipa, had been named executor, or she supposed executrix, of the estate of one Pierce Inverarity, a California real estate mogul who had once lost two million dollars in his spare time but still had assets numerous and tangled enough to make the job of sorting it all out more than honorary.

Thomas Pynchon, *The Crying of Lot 49*

From a little after two oclock until almost sundown of the long still hot weary dead September afternoon they sat in what Miss Coldfield still called the office because her father had called it that—a dim hot airless room with the blinds all closed and fastened for forty-three summers because when she was a girl someone had believed that light and moving air carried heat and that dark was always cooler, and which (as the sun shone fuller and fuller on that side of the house) became latticed with yellow slashes full of dust motes which Quentin thought of as being flecks of the dead old dried paint itself blown inward from the scaling blinds as wind might have blown them.

William Faulkner, *Absalom, Absalom!*

Our eyes register the light of dead stars.

André Schwarz-Bart, *The Last of the Just*

My true name is so well known in the records or registers at Newgate, and in the Old Bailey, and there are some things of such consequence still depending there, relating to my particular conduct, that it is not to be expected I should set my name or the account of my family to this work; perhaps, after my death, it may be better known; at present it would not be proper, no, not though a general pardon should be issued, even without exceptions and reserve of persons or crimes.

Daniel Defoe, *Moll Flanders*

It is a trite but true observation that examples work more forcibly on the mind than precepts, and if this be just in what is odious and blameable, it is more strongly so in what is amiable and praiseworthy.

Henry Fielding, *Joseph Andrews*

The Mole had been working very hard all the morning, spring-cleaning his little home.

Kenneth Grahame, *The Wind in the Willows*

The day had gone by just as days go by.

Hermann Hesse, *Steppenwolf*

The sun shone, having no alternative, on the nothing new.

Samuel Beckett, *Murphy*

No, no, I can't tell you everything.

Primo Levi, *The Monkey's Wrench*

You tell.

Günter Grass, *Dog Years*

Weidmann appeared before you in a five o'clock edition, his head swathed in white bands, a nun and yet a wounded pilot fallen into the rye one September day like the day when the world came to know the name of Our Lady of the Flowers.

Jean Genet, *Our Lady of the Flowers*

Vadinho, Dona Floor's first husband, died one Sunday of Carnival, in the morning, when dressed up like a Bahian woman, he was dancing the samba, with the greatest enthusiasm, in the Dois de Julho Square, not far from his house.

Jorge Amado, *Dona Floor and Her Two Husbands*

—Something a little strange, that's what you notice, that she's not a woman like all the others.

Manuel Puig, *Kiss of the Spider Woman*

The tradesmen of Bridgepoint learned to dread the sound of "Miss Mathilda," for with that name the good Anna always conquered.

Gertrude Stein, *Three Lives*

Samuel Spade's jaw was long and bony, his chin a jutting v under the more flexible v of his mouth.

Dorothy L. Sayers, *Strong Poison*

The bench on which Dobbs was sitting was not so good.

B. Traven, *The Treasure of the Sierra Madre*

There was only one bench in the shade and Converse went for it, although it was already occupied.

Robert Stone, *Dog Soldiers*

Through the fence, between the curling flower spaces,
I could see them hitting.

William Faulkner, *The Sound and the Fury*

The boys, as they talked to the girls from Marcia Blaine
School, stood on the far side of their bicycles holding the
handlebars, which established a protective fence of bicycle
between the sexes, and the impression that any moment the
boys were likely to be away.

Muriel Spark, *The Prime of Miss Jean Brodie*

I went back to the Devon School not long ago, and
found it looking oddly newer than when I was a student there
fifteen years before.

John Knowles, *A Separate Peace*

Though brilliantly sunny, Saturday morning was overcoat weather again, not just topcoat weather, as it had been
all week, and as everyone had hoped it would stay for the big
weekend—the weekend of the Yale game.

J. D. Salinger, *Franny and Zooey*

It was dolphin weather, when I sailed into Piraeus with
my comrades of the Cretan bull ring.

Mary Renault, *The Bull from the Sea*

The boy with fair hair lowered himself down the last few
feet of rock and began to pick his way toward the lagoon.

William Golding, *The Lord of the Flies*

The sea is high again today, with a thrilling flush
of wind.

Lawrence Durrell, *Justine*

Ships at a distance have every man's wish on board.

Zora Neale Hurston, *Their Eyes Were Watching God*

A wide plain, where the broadening Floss hurries on between its green banks to the sea, and the loving tide, rushing to meet it, checks its passage with an impetuous embrace.

George Eliot, *The Mill on the Floss*

The *Nellie*, a cruising yawl, swung to her anchor without a flutter of the sails, and was at rest.

Joseph Conrad, *Heart of Darkness*

One January day, thirty years ago, the little town of Hanover, anchored on a windy Nebraska tableland, was trying not to be blown away.

Willa Cather, *O Pioneers!*

On a cold blowy February day a woman is boarding the ten a.m. flight to London, followed by an invisible dog.

Alison Lurie, *Foreign Affairs*

It was clearly going to be a bad crossing.

Evelyn Waugh, *Vile Bodies*

There was a depression over the Atlantic.

Robert Musil, *The Man Without Qualities*

It might be most dramatically effective to begin the tale at the moment when Arnold Baffin rang me up and said, "Bradley, could you come round here please, I think that I have just killed my wife."

Iris Murdoch, *The Black Prince*

My dear friends, I knew you were faithful.

André Gide, *The Immoralist*

"I see …" said the vampire thoughtfully, and slowly he walked across the room towards the window.

Anne Rice, *Interview with the Vampire*

Mr. Utterson the lawyer was a man of a rugged countenance that was never lighted by a smile; cold, scanty and embarrassed in discourse; backward in sentiment; lean, long, dusty, dreary and yet somehow loveable.

Robert Louis Stevenson, *The Strange Case of Dr. Jekyll and Mr. Hyde*

There lived in Westphalia, in the castle of the Baron of Thunder-Ten-Tronckh, a young man on whom nature had bestowed the perfection of gentle manners.

Voltaire, *Candide*

In a hole in the ground there lived a hobbit.

J. R. R. Tolkien, *The Hobbit*

A green hunting cap squeezed the top of the fleshy balloon of a head.

John Kennedy Toole, *A Confederacy of Dunces*

Miss Brooke had that kind of beauty which seems to be thrown into relief by poor dress.

George Eliot, *Middlemarch*

Scarlett O'Hara was not beautiful, but men seldom realized it when caught by her charm as the Tarleton twins were.

Margaret Mitchell, *Gone with the Wind*

Here we are, alone again.

Louis-Ferdinand Céline, *Death on the Installment Plan*

In the town there were two mutes, and they were always together.

Carson McCullers, *The Heart Is a Lonely Hunter*

I am writing this because people I love have died.

Amos Oz, *My Michael*

Mother died today. Or was it yesterday?

Albert Camus, *The Stranger*

My first act on entering this world was to kill my mother.

William Boyd, *The New Confession*

She was so deeply imbedded in my consciousness that for the first year of school I seem to have believed that each of my teachers was my mother in disguise.

Philip Roth, *Portnoy's Complaint*

For a short while during the year I was ten, I thought only people I did not know died.

Jamaica Kincaid, *Annie John*

On top of everything, the cancer wing was Number 13.

Alexander Solzhenitsyn, *The Cancer Ward*

Marley was dead, to begin with.

Charles Dickens, *A Christmas Carol*

Died on me finally.

Allan Gurganus, *Oldest Living Confederate Widow Tells All*

And so they've killed our Ferdinand, said the charwoman to Mr. Svejk, who had left military service years before, after having been finally certified by an army medical board as an imbecile, and now lived by selling dogs—ugly, mongrel, monstrosities whose pedigrees he forged.

Jaroslav Jašek, *The Good Soldier Švejk*

Riding up the winding road of Saint Agnes Cemetery in the back of the rattling old truck, Francis Phelan became aware that the dead, even more than the living, settled down in neighborhoods.

William Kennedy, *Ironweed*

I am always drawn back to places where I have lived, the houses and their neighborhoods.

Truman Capote, *Breakfast at Tiffany's*

Half-way down a by-street of one of our New England towns, stands a rusty wooden house, with seven acutely peaked gables facing towards various points of the compass, and a huge, clustered chimney in the midst.

Nathaniel Hawthorne, *The House of Seven Gables*

The towers of Zenith aspired above the morning Mist; austere towers of steel and cement and limestone, sturdy as cliffs and delicate as silver rods.

Sinclair Lewis, *Babbitt*

A squat grey building of only thirty-four stories.

Aldous Huxley, *Brave New World*

In those days cheap apartments were almost impossible to find in Manhattan, so I had to move to Brooklyn.

William Styron, *Sophie's Choice*

Serene was a word you could put to Brooklyn, New York.

Betty Smith, *A Tree Grows in Brooklyn*

It was a queer, sultry summer, the summer they electrocuted the Rosenbergs, and I didn't know what I was doing in New York.

Sylvia Plath, *The Bell Jar*

So great was the noise during the day that I used to lie awake at night listening to silence.

Muriel Spark, *A Far Cry from Kensington*

Nobody could sleep.

Norman Mailer, *The Naked and the Dead*

"What's it going to be then, eh?"

Anthony Burgess, *A Clockwork Orange*

There was a time when people were in the habit of addressing themselves frequently and felt no shame at making a record of their inward transactions.

Saul Bellow, *Dangling Man*

The cabin-passenger wrote in his diary a parody of Descartes: "I feel discomfort, therefore I am alive," then sat pen in hand with no more to record.

Graham Greene, *A Burnt-Out Case*

Elmer Gantry was drunk.

Sinclair Lewis, *Elmer Gantry*

All children, except one, grow up.

James M. Barrie, *Peter Pan*

It was a pleasure to burn.

Ray Bradbury, *Fahrenheit 451*

The oyster leads a dreadful but exciting life.

M. F. K. Fisher, *Consider the Oyster*

Until I was 8 years I had no thought of getting married. I was seduced on our front lawn and my mother and father were watching.

Richard Armour, *My Life with Women*

He—for there could be no doubt of his sex, though the fashion of the time did something to disguise it—was in the act of slicing at the head of a Moor which swung from the rafters.

Virginia Woolf, *Orlando*

Armory Blain inherited from his mother every trait, except the stray inexpressible few, that made him worth while.

F. Scott Fitzgerald, *This Side of Paradise*

It was to have been a quiet evening at home.

John D. Mac Donald, *The Deep Blue Good-by*

There once was a boy by the name of Eustace Clarence Scrubb, and he almost deserved it.

C. S. Lewis, *The Voyage of the Dawn Treader*

The cradle rocks above an abyss, and common sense tells us that our existence is but a brief crack of light between two eternities of darkness.

Vladimir Nabokov, *Speak Memory*

As Gregor Samsa awoke one morning from uneasy dreams he found himself transformed in his bed into a gigantic insect.

Franz Kafka, "Metamorphosis"

Now at last the slowly gathered, long-pent-up fury of the storm broke upon us.

Winston Churchill, *Their Finest Hour*

"Hide the Christmas tree carefully, Helen."

Henrik Ibsen, *A Doll's House*

"Make it fast."

Eugene O'Neill, *The Iceman Cometh*

On January 6, 1482, the people of Paris were awakened by the tumultuous clanging of all the bells in the city.

Victor Hugo, *The Hunchback of Notre Dame*

"Tush; never tell me."

William Shakespeare, *Othello*

When Mary Lennox was sent to Misselthwaite Manor to live with her uncle everybody said she was the most disagreeable-looking child ever seen.

Frances Hodgson Burnett, *The Secret Garden*

There was death at its beginning as there would be death again at its end.

Nicholas Evans, *The Horse Whisperer*

They were supposed to stay at the beach a week, but neither of them had the heart for it and they decided to come back early.

Anne Tyler, *The Accidental Tourist*

What a liar and a hypocrite I've become.

Rita Mae Brown, *Dolley*

On the desk in my candlelit study, the telephone rang, and I knew that a terrible change was coming.

Dean R. Koontz, *Fear Nothing*

Everyone now knows how to find the meaning of life within himself.

Kurt Vonnegut, *The Sirens of Titan*

This is the tale of a meeting of two lonesome, skinny, fairly old white men on a planet which was dying fast.

Kurt Vonnegut, *Breakfast of Champions*

While Pearl Tull was dying, a funny thought occurred to her.

Anne Tyler, *Dinner at the Homesick Restaurant*

The silence woke her.

Mary Jo Putney, *The Bartered Bride*

A clock ticked loudly in the hall as Gabriella Harrison stood silently in the utter darkness of the closet.

Danielle Steel, *The Long Road Home*

We are at rest five miles behind the front.

Erich Maria Remarque, *All Quiet on the Western Front*

It was about eleven o'clock in the morning, mid October, with the sun not shining and a look of hard wet rain in the clearness of the foothills.

Raymond Chandler, *The Big Sleep*

On a January evening of the early seventies, Christine Nilsson was singing in Faust at the Academy of Music in New York.

Edith Wharton, *The Age of Innocence*

The family of Dashwood had long been settled in Sussex.

Jane Austen, *Sense and Sensibility*

No one who had ever seen Catherine Moreland in her infancy would have supposed her born to be a heroine.

Jane Austen, *Northanger Abbey*

Midway upon the journey of our life I found myself in a dark wilderness, for I had wandered from the straight and true.

Dante, *Inferno*

There was no possibility of taking a walk that day.

Charlotte Bronte, *Jane Eyre*

Jeeves—my man, you know—is really a most extraordinary chap.

P. G. Wodehouse, *My Man Jeeves*

It is a sin to write this.

Ayn Rand, *Anthem*

John Kurtz, the chief of the Boston police, breathed in some of his heft for a better fit between the two chambermaids.

Matthew Pearl, *The Dante Club*

To Sherlock Holmes she is always *the* woman.

Sir Arthur Conan Doyle, *The Adventures of Sherlock Holmes*

He should never have taken that shortcut.

Michael Crichton, *Timeline*

The idiot lived in a black and gray world, punctuated by the white lightening of hunger and the flickering of fear.

Theodore Sturgeon, *More than Human*

Ever since Genevieve Terrence's mama had inherited a pair of Elvis's Jockey shorts, Genevieve had been a big believer in luck.

Vicki Lewis Thompson, *Nerd in Shining Armor*

Once a guy stood all day shaking bugs from his hair.

Philip K. Dick, *A Scanner Darkly*

Billy Ray Cobb was the younger and smaller of the two rednecks.

John Grisham, *A Time to Kill*

The year 1866 was signalized by a remarkable incident, a mysterious and puzzling phenomenon, which doubtless no one has yet forgotten.

Jules Verne, *20,000 Leagues Under the Sea*

Mr. Sherlock Holmes, who was usually very late in the mornings, save upon those not infrequent occasions when he was up all night, was seated at the breakfast table.

Sir Arthur Conan Doyle, *Hound of the Baskervilles*

"Tell me about the thumb."

Robert Crais, *Demolition Angel*

Mortal fear is knowing you've been poisoned.

Jeff Abbott, *Distant Blood*

One may as well begin with Meg's letters to her sister.

E. M. Forster, *Howards End*

"Christmas won't be Christmas without any presents," grumbled Jo, lying on the rug.

Louisa May Alcott, *Little Women*

The schoolmaster was leaving the village, and everyone seemed sorry.

Thomas Hardy, *Jude the Obscure*

"CAMELOT—Camelot," said I to myself.

Mark Twain, *A Connecticut Yankee in King Arthur's Court*

"Gregory, on my word, we'll not carry coals."

William Shakespeare, *Romeo and Juliet*

She hasn't been dead four months and I've already eaten to the bottom of the deep freeze.

Kaye Gibbons, *A Virtuous Woman*

Ahab was neither my first husband nor my last.

Sena Jeeter Nasland, *Ahab's Wife*

...a stone, a leaf, an unfound door; of a stone, a leaf, a door. And of all the forgotten faces.

Thomas Wolfe, *Look Homeward, Angel*

You never meant to kill him.

Harlan Coben, *The Innocent*

The cop climbed out of his car exactly four minutes before he got shot. He moved like he knew his fate in advance.

Lee Child, *Persuader*

Marianne nursed her third shot of Cuervo, marveling at her endless capacity to destroy any good in her pathetic life, when the man next to her shouted, "Listen up, sweetcakes: Creationism and evolution are totally compatible."

His spittle landed on Marianne's neck.

Harlan Coben, *Hold Tight*

For an ending to this book let us get away from the great succinct one-liners and go to a flamboyant and self-indulgent beginning to a famous and highly influential story of the 1930s and 1940s: "The Daring Young Man on the Flying Trapeze" by William Saroyan. One weekend in 1933 my older brother brought the unknown writer to our home from a bar.

"I have just written a *great* story!" he boomed. "It will make me famous!"

And so it did.

Here are the first paragraphs:

I. SLEEP

Horizontally wakeful amid universal widths, practicing laughter and mirth, satire, the end of all, of Rome and yes of Babylon, clenched teeth, remembrance, much warmth volcanic, the streets of Paris, the plains of Jericho, much gliding as of reptile in abstraction, a gallery of watercolors, the sea and the fish with eyes, symphony, a table in the corner of the Eiffel Tower, jazz at the opera house, alarm clock and tap-dancing of doom, conversation with a tree, the river Nile, Cadillac coupé to Kansas, the roar of Dostoyevsky, and the dark sun.

This earth, the face of one who lived, the form without the weight, weeping upon snow, white music, the magnified flower twice the size of the universe, black clouds, the caged panther staring, deathless space, Mr. Eliot with rolled sleeves baking bread, Flaubert and Guy de Maupassant, a wordless rhyme of early meaning, Finlandia, mathematics highly polished and slick as a green onion to the teeth, Jerusalem, the path to paradox.

The deep song of man, the sly whisper of someone un-seen but vaguely known, hurricane in the cornfield, a game of chess, hush the queen, the king, Karl Franz, black Titanic, Mr. Chaplin weeping, Stalin, Hitler, a multitude of Jews, tomorrow is Monday, no dancing in the streets.

O swift moment of life: it is ended, the earth is again now.

Whew!

And, so like Saroyan's swift moment of life, our book on beginnings has its end.

The End

Index

Barnaby Conrad

An O. Henry Prize short story winner, he has written thirty books, including the bestsellers *Matador*, *Dangerfield* and *La Fiesta Brava*. The previous book in his writing series was *101 Best Scenes Ever Written*. Born in San Francisco, he served as American Vice Consul in Spain during World War II. As an amateur bullfighter he performed in Spain, Mexico and Peru over some fifteen years until badly gored in El Escorial, Spain. As a young man he worked as secretary to the novelist Sinclair Lewis in Williamstown, Massachusetts. He wrote a "Playhouse 90" script for John Frankenheimer, the screenplay for Steinbeck's *Flight*, and a Broadway play from his novel *Dangerfield*. He is the founder of the prestigious Santa Barbara Writers Conference, now in its thirty-sixth year.

Of his latest novel, *Last Boat to Cadiz*, William F. Buckley has written: "A master storyteller has done it again with a great tale."

1/3/2011   8/31/2015   18   2